WAR
OF THE
WORLDVIEWS

POWERFUL ANSWERS FOR AN "EVOLUTIONIZED" CULTURE

KEN HAM | BODIE HODGE | CARL KERBY | DR. JASON LISLE
| STACIA MCKEEVER | DR. DAVID MENTON | DR. TERRY
MORTENSON | DR. GEORGIA PURDOM | MIKE RIDDLE

EDITED & COMPILED BY GARY VATERLAUS

answersingenesis.org
believing it. defending it. proclaiming it.

For more information, write
Answers in Genesis, PO Box 510, Hebron, KY 41048
1-800-350-3232 • www.AnswersInGenesis.org

ISBN 1-893345-71-8

Cover design: Brandie Lucas
Interior layout: Diane King
Editors: Becky Stelzer, Stacia McKeever & Michael Matthews

Printed in the United States of America

TABLE OF CONTENTS

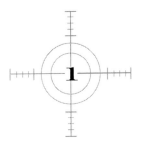

THE "EVOLUTIONIZING" OF A CULTURE

CARL KERBY & KEN HAM

As you picked up this book, you may have asked yourself, "Why should I care about this stuff? What do "worldviews" have to do with me? Who cares about astronomy and biology? Who cares about mutations and the big bang? What does any of this have to do with real life? These are all just side issues; don't we have more important things to worry about, like evangelism and caring for the needy?" We're glad you're asking these kinds of questions. Our society is engaged in a culture war: the Left versus the Right, pro-choice versus pro-life, etc. You see it every day on the network news and in the newspapers. But what is the foundational issue behind all of these battles? How can we reach people engaged in these culture wars with the truth? In this chapter we will examine the true nature of this war and see how a return to biblical authority in the church, particularly as it relates to Genesis and creation, is crucial to winning the war of the worldviews.

WE ARE ENGAGED IN A war of worldviews. Secular humanism (with its evolutionary and millions-of-years foundation) is fighting tooth-and-nail against biblical Christianity (and the idea that God is the Creator) for the hearts and minds of our children. Over the past generations, we've seen the battle increase and intensify.

There's no doubt America was founded on Christian principles based on the Bible. In fact, just two generations ago, the majority of Americans supported prayer, Scripture readings and Bible instruction in public schools. They also supported dis-

playing nativity scenes, crosses and the Ten Commandments in public places. Gay marriage and abortion were outlawed.

Today, however, it is very obvious that the population as a whole does not see the Bible as the absolute authority as it once did. For instance, pollster George Barna found that in the US "a minority of born again adults (44%) and an even smaller proportion of born again teenagers (9%) are certain of the existence of absolute moral truth."[1]

So what has happened? Why the dramatic change? Why is the moral position of previous generations being outlawed more and more? What has driven this moral collapse? Why is this war going on?

Whereas Christian thinking once permeated the public education system, today the Christian God, prayer, Bible study and biblical creation have all but been excluded from the system.

---

[1]   Barna Research Online, The year's most intriguing findings, from Barna Research Studies, December 12, 2000.

Now, generations (including the majority of students from church homes) are being trained in a secular (anti-God) religion.[2] They are being indoctrinated to believe that the universe—and all that exists within it—can be explained without God.

They are taught, with increasing intensity, a cosmology, geology, biology and anthropology that are all evolutionary. In essence, these students are being educated *against* the truth of the Bible's history in Genesis, and thus, against its message of salvation and absolute moral standards.

Not only are our schools indoctrinating our children, but so are the media. Television shows, movies, comic books, ads and so on are all laced with evolutionary thought, subtly (and not-so-subtly) reinforcing the idea that we are nothing but evolved pond scum, the result of billions of years of natural processes.

Just a few examples of this should suffice: the more highly evolved X-Men and the "millions of years" taught in *Jurassic Park* and *Dinosaurs*. Magazines such as *Time*, *Nature* and *National Geographic* often have cover stories touting evolution as fact. And who can ignore the many cable channels, such as Discovery Channel, The Learning Channel and Animal Planet, which regularly broadcast shows on animal and human evolution?

American children, ages 2 to 17, spend an average of 19.4 hours watching TV each week (Nielsen Media Research, 2000). And this doesn't include the time spent going to movies, playing computer games, surfing the internet or reading comic books and magazines. Our children are inundated with messages from the media, which by and large have an evolutionary, anti-Christian foundation.

---

[2] There is no such thing as neutrality. As the Bible states in Matthew 12:30: "He that is not with me is against me; and he that gathereth not with me scattereth abroad."

In the United States, we have approximately 400,000 churches and 6,000 first-run theaters. Which do you think affects our culture more? Unfortunately, the Hollywood writers and producers have more influence on our youth today than our pastors and Sunday school teachers.

CHRISTIAN COMPROMISE

Sadly, most Christian leaders in the church have added ammunition to the other side by compromising with evolutionary ideas (either wittingly or unwittingly); they have added millions of years to the Bible, and many teach that evolution and Christianity are compatible. These leaders have, in effect, helped this takeover and fueled the culture war. What has resulted is that recent generations have begun to reject or rein-

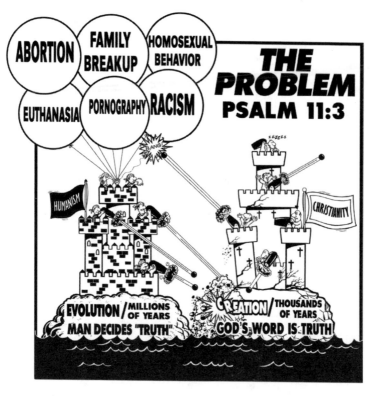

terpret the Bible's history in Genesis, thus opening a door to undermine biblical authority in general for the other 65 books of the Bible.

The more that generations are trained to disbelieve the Bible's account of origins, the more they will doubt the rest of the Bible, as all biblical doctrines (including marriage) are founded (directly or indirectly) in the history in Genesis 1–11. We see the direct result of this doubt and compromise reflected in the increasing number of moral battles concerning gay marriage, abortion and so on. Again, the more people believe evolution and reject Genesis 1–11 as history, the more they will reject the rest of the Bible—including the morality that is based in that history.

Secularism, with its moral relativism, is in direct opposition to Christianity and its absolute morality. The battle is between these two worldviews: one which stands on God's Word and one which accepts man's opinions.

What will be the outcome? Can America return to a Christian worldview that will once again permeate the culture? Yes, it can, but only if there is a return to the authority of the Word of God ... beginning in Genesis.

AMMUNITION FOR THE BATTLE

In the following chapters, you will find valuable information to equip you to understand the nature of the battle and to answer the evolutionists' latest arguments.

Chapter 2 deals with the Miller-Urey experiment of the 1950s that tried to produce the building blocks of life in a laboratory; science textbooks still refer to it today. See why the experiment fails at all levels and why it is impossible for life and information to arise by purely naturalistic processes.

Chapter 3 examines mutations—what they are and how they work. Find out why they cannot be the "engine" of evolution.

In chapter 4 we will look at supposed human evolution. By examining the actual evidence, we will see that there are no "missing links" between chimps and humans, just monkey (or ape) fossils and human fossils. Humans are truly unique creations, made in the image of God.

Chapters 5 and 6 consider astronomy. Is the big bang biblical? Does the Bible support modern-day cosmological theories? See how the Bible is truly the history book of the universe and is accurate when it touches on astronomical concepts.

The topic of chapter 7 is the history of geological thought. We examine where the idea of "millions of years" came from and the disastrous consequences of the church's acceptance of evolutionary ages.

Chapters 8 and 9 take a critical look at the Progressive Creation and Intelligent Design movements. Are these biblical approaches to creation? What happens when we mix evolutionary thought with the Bible?

Many evolutionary scientists have stated that creationists cannot be real scientists. Is this true? See why this is not the case in chapter 10.

We also deal with the troubling issue of "gay marriage." Does the Bible have anything to say about this? How is evolution connected to this issue? Read chapter 11 and find out how to give a biblical answer for these and other moral issues of our day.

Chapter 12 discusses the "proofs" of creation. We need to understand the nature of "evidence" and how our presuppositions affect our interpretations. This is a foundational message in the creation/evolution controversy.

And finally we come to the biblical view of history—the 7 C's of history—in chapter 13. A truly biblical understanding of history helps us understand the rest of the world and helps us put the evidence where it belongs.

WINNING THE WAR

We cannot just tell people, "Jesus loves you and has a wonderful plan for your life." The world has questions and we need to give them answers. We need to show skeptics that the Bible relates to the real world—that a biblical worldview addresses biology, astronomy, history and anthropology. We need to help our children build their worldview on the Bible and equip them with answers for their teachers and friends. We need to take action to halt the desertion

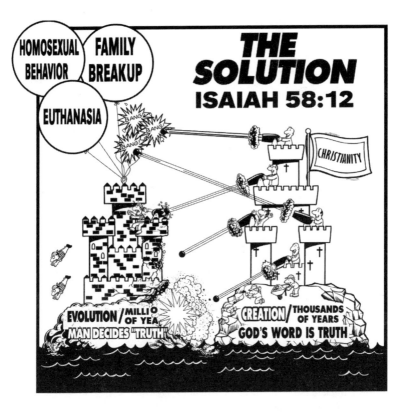

of children from their faith after they leave home.[3]

Christians who are fighting for a return to biblical morality cannot hope to win the "war of the worldviews" and will only continue to see the erosion of this once-Christian culture unless they understand the real foundational nature of the battle: biblical authority, beginning with God's Word in Genesis, must be upheld without compromise.

The secular world itself understands the battle—but the church by and large does not. Christian leaders need to be awakened by a battle cry. We need to attack the false foundation of evolution and millions of years and proclaim the true history of the world that is foundational to Christian morality and the gospel of Jesus Christ.

---

[3] It is estimated by the Barna Institute that in this generation two-thirds of the children from evangelical homes will leave the church after they leave home. For more information, see *State of the Church: 2002* by George Barna.

CAN NATURAL PROCESSES EXPLAIN THE ORIGIN OF LIFE?

MIKE RIDDLE

Have you seen the movie *Mission to Mars*? Astronauts discover that the "seeds of life" were planted on Earth billions of years ago by an alien race that once lived on Mars. After a meteor destroyed the atmosphere of Mars, these aliens left to colonize a distant planet, but not without first leaving DNA on Earth, which began the process of evolution. Realizing the remote possibility of life spontaneously beginning on Earth, some evolutionary scientists, including the codiscoverer of the structure of DNA, Francis Crick, have proposed that life began on Earth from material that had come from outer space. However, moving the origin of life to another planet does not solve the problem. Could simple life have arisen on Earth or any other planet? What would be involved in such a process? In this chapter, we examine the origin of life and see that only the Bible explains it: "In the beginning God created ..." (Genesis 1:1).

W HEN CONSIDERING HOW LIFE BEGAN, there are only two options. Either life was created by an intelligent source (God) or it began by natural processes. The common perception presented in many textbooks and in the media is that life arose from nonlife in a pool of chemicals about 3.8 billion years ago. The claim by evolutionists is that this formation of life was the result of time, chance and natural processes. One widely used example of how life could have formed by natural processes is the Miller-Urey experiment, performed in the early 1950s.

Miller's objective was not to create life but to simulate how life's basic building structures (amino acids[1]) might have formed in the early earth. In the experiment, Miller attempted to simulate the early atmosphere of Earth by using certain gases, which he thought might produce organic compounds necessary for life. Since the gases he included (water, methane, ammonia and hydrogen) do not react with each other under natural conditions, he generated electrical currents to simulate some form of energy input (such as lightning) that was needed to drive the chemical reactions. The result was production of amino acids. Many textbooks promote this experiment as the first step in explaining how life could have originated. But there is more to this experiment than what is commonly represented in textbooks.

THE REST OF THE STORY—SOME CRITICAL THINKING

When we examine the purpose, assumptions and results of the Miller experiment, there are three critical thinking questions that can be raised:

---

[1] The basic building blocks of all living systems are proteins, which consist of only twenty different types of amino acids. The average number of amino acids in a biological protein is over 300. These amino acids must be arranged in a very specific sequence for each protein.

1. How much of the experiment was left to chance processes or how much involved intelligent design?

2. How did Miller know what Earth's early atmosphere (billions of years ago) was like?

3. Did Miller produce the right type of amino acids used in life?

THE METHOD USED

In the experiment, Miller was attempting to illustrate how life's building blocks (amino acids) could have formed by natural processes. However, throughout the experiment Miller relied on years of intelligent research in chemistry. He purposely chose which gases to include and which to exclude. Next, he had to isolate the biochemicals (amino acids) from the environment he had creted them in because it would have destroyed them. No such

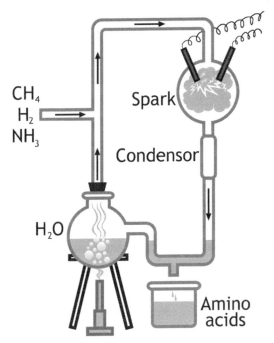

CH_4
H_2
NH_3

Spark

Condensor

H_2O

Amino acids

system would have existed on the so-called "primitive" earth. It appears Miller used intelligent design throughout the experiment rather than chance processes.

THE STARTING INGREDIENTS

How did Miller know what the atmosphere was like billions of years ago? Miller assumed that the early earth's atmosphere was very different from today. He based his starting chemical mixture on the assumption that the early earth had a reducing atmosphere (an atmosphere that contains no free oxygen). Why did Miller and many other evolutionists assume there was no free oxygen in Earth's early atmosphere? As attested below, it is well known that biological molecules (specifically amino acid bonds) are destroyed in the presence of oxygen, making it impossible for life to evolve.

> Oxygen is a poisonous gas that oxidizes organic and inorganic materials on a planetary surface; it is quite lethal to organisms that have not evolved protection against it.[2]

> … in the atmosphere and in the various water basins of the primitive earth, many destructive interactions would have so vastly diminished, if not altogether consumed, essential precursor chemicals, that chemical evolution rates would have been negligible.[3]

Therefore, in order to avoid this problem, evolutionists propose that Earth's first atmosphere did not contain any freestand-

---

[2] Ward, P., and Brownlee, D., *Rare Earth*, p. 245, 2000.
[3] Thaxton, C., Bradley, W., and Olsen, R., *The Mystery of Life's Origin: Reassessing Current Theories*, p. 66, 1984.

ing oxygen. We must ask ourselves, "Is there any evidence to support this claim, or is it based on the assumption that evolution must be true?" As it turns out, the existence of a reducing atmosphere is merely an assumption not supported by the physical evidence. The evidence points to the fact that the earth has always had oxygen in the atmosphere.

> There is no scientific proof that Earth ever had a non-oxygen atmosphere such as evolutionists require. Earth's oldest rocks contain evidence of being formed in an oxygen atmosphere.[4]

> The only trend in the recent literature is the suggestion of far more oxygen in the early atmosphere than anyone imagined.[5]

If we were to grant the evolutionists' assumption of no oxygen in the original atmosphere, another fatal problem arises. Since the ozone is made of oxygen, it would not exist; and the ultraviolet rays from the sun would destroy any biological molecules. This presents a no-win situation for the evolution model. If there was oxygen, life could not start. If there was no oxygen, life could not start. Michael Denton notes:

> What we have is sort of a "Catch 22" situation. If we have oxygen we have no organic compounds, but if we don't have oxygen we have none either.[6]

---

[4] Clemmey, H., and Badham, N., Oxygen in the atmosphere: an evaluation of the geological evidence, *Geology* **10**:141, 1982.
[5] Thaxton, C., Bradley, W., and Olsen, R., *The Mystery of Life's Origin*, p. 80, 1992.
[6] Denton, M., *Evolution: A Theory in Crisis*, p. 261, 1985.

Because life could not have originated on land, some evolutionists propose that life started in the oceans. The problem with life starting in the oceans, however, is that as organic molecules formed, the water would have immediately destroyed them through a process called *hydrolysis*. Hydrolysis, which means "water splitting," is the addition of a water molecule between two bonded molecules (two amino acids in this case), which causes them to split apart. Many scientists have noted this problem.

> Besides breaking up polypeptides, hydrolysis would have destroyed many amino acids.[7]

> In general the half-lives of these polymers in contact with water are on the order of days and months—time spans which are surely geologically insignificant.[8]

> Furthermore, water tends to break chains of amino acids apart. If any proteins had formed in the oceans 3.5 billion years ago, they would have quickly disintegrated.[9]

Scientifically, there is no known solution for how life could have chemically evolved on the earth.

ON THE OTHER HAND ...

Because the scientific evidence contradicts the origin of life by natural processes, Miller resorted to unrealistic initial conditions to develop amino acids in his experiment (no oxygen and excessive energy input). However, there is more to the story. Producing amino acids is not the hard part. The difficult part is get-

---

[7]　Encyclopedia of Science and Technology, Vol. 1, pp. 411-412, 1982.
[8]　Dose, K., *The Origin of Life and Evolutionary Biochemistry*, p. 69, 1974.
[9]　Morris, R., *The Big Questions*, p. 167, 2002.

ting the right type and organization of amino acids. There are over 2,000 types of amino acids, but only 20 are used in life. Furthermore, the atoms which make up each amino acid are assembled in two basic shapes. These are known as *left-handed* and *right-handed*. Compare them to human hands. Each hand has the same components (four fingers and a thumb), yet they are different. The thumb of one hand is on the left, and the thumb of the other is on the right. They are mirror images of each other. Like our hands, amino acids come in two shapes. They are composed of the same atoms (components) but are mirror images of each other, called left-handed amino acids and right-handed amino acids. Objects that have handedness are said to be chiral (pronounced "ky-rul"), which is from the Greek for "hand."

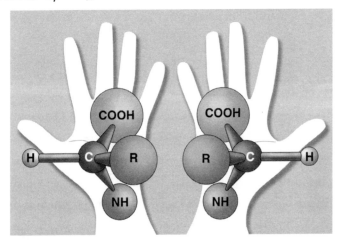

Handedness is an important concept because all amino acids that make up proteins in living things are 100% left-handed. Right-handed amino acids are never found in proteins. If a protein were assembled with just one right-handed amino acid, the protein's function would be totally lost. As one Ph.D. chemist has said,

> Many of life's chemicals come in two forms, "left-handed" and "right-handed." Life requires polymers with all building blocks having the same "handedness" (*homochirality*)—proteins have only "left-handed" amino acids ... . But ordinary undirected chemistry, as is the hypothetical primordial soup, would produce equal mixtures of left- and right-handed molecules, called *racemates*.[10]

A basic chemistry textbook admits,

> This is a very puzzling fact ... . All the proteins that have been investigated, obtained from animals and from plants from higher organisms and from very simple organisms—bacteria, molds, even viruses—are found to have been made of L-amino [left-handed] acids.[11]

The common perception left by many textbooks and journals is that Miller and other scientists were successful in producing the amino acids necessary for life. However, the textbooks and media fail to mention that what they had actually produced was a mixture of left- and right-handed amino acids, which is detrimental to life. The natural tendency is for left- and right-handed amino acids to bond together. Scientist still do not know why biological proteins use only left-handed amino acids.

---

[10] Sarfati, J., *In Six Days*, p. 82, 2000.
[11] Pauling, L., *General Chemistry*, Third Edition, p. 774, 1970.

The reason for this choice [only left-handed amino acids] is again a mystery, and a subject of continuous dispute.[12]

Jonathan Wells, a developmental biologist, writes,

So we remain profoundly ignorant of how life originated. Yet the Miller-Urey experiment continues to be used as an icon of evolution, because nothing better has turned up. Instead of being told the truth, we are given the misleading impression that scientists have empirically demonstrated the first step in the origin of life.[13]

Despite the fact that the Miller experiment did not succeed in creating the building blocks of life (only left-handed amino acids), textbooks continue to promote the idea that life could have originated by natural processes. For example, the following statement from a biology textbook misleads students into thinking Miller succeeded:

By re-creating the early atmosphere (ammonia, water, hydrogen and methane) and passing an electric spark (lightning) through the mixture, Miller and Urey proved that organic matter such as amino acids could have formed spontaneously.[14]

First, note the word "proved." Miller and Urey proved nothing except that life's building blocks could *not* form in such conditions. Second, the textbook completely ignores other evidence,

[12] Shapiro, R., *Origins*, p. 86, 1986.
[13] Wells, J., *Icons of Evolution*, p. 24, 2000.
[14] Miller, K., and Levine, J., *Biology*, 2000.

which shows that the atmosphere always contained oxygen. Third, the textbook ignores the fact that Miller got the wrong type of amino acids—a mixture of left- and right-handed.

The Miller experiment (and all experiments since then) failed to produce even a single biological protein by purely naturalistic processes. Only God could have begun life.

INFORMATION

Another important component of life is information. The common factor in all living organisms is the information contained in their cells. Where and how did all this coded information arise? Proteins are amazingly versatile and carry out many biochemical functions, but they are incapable of assembling themselves without the assistance of DNA. The function of DNA is to store information and pass it on (transcribe) to RNA, while the function of RNA is to read, decode and use the information received from DNA to make proteins. Each of the thousands of genes on a DNA molecule contains instructions necessary to make specific proteins that, in turn, are needed for specific biological functions.

Any hypothesis or model meant to explain how all life evolved from lifeless chemicals into a complex cell consisting of vast amounts of information also has to explain the source of information and how this information was encoded into the genome. All evolutionary explanations are unable to answer this question. Dr. Werner Gitt, former physics professor and director of information processing at the Institute of Physics and Technology in Braunschweig, Germany, and Dr. Lee Spetner both agree that information cannot arise by naturalistic processes:

There is no known law of nature, no known process and no known sequence of events which can cause information to originate by itself in matter.[15]

Not even one mutation has been observed that adds a little information to the genome. This surely shows that there are not the millions upon millions of potential mutations the theory [evolution] demands.[16]

The DNA code within all plant and animal cells is vastly more compact than any computer chip ever made. DNA is so compact that a one-square-inch chip of DNA could encode the information in over 7 billion Bibles. Since the density and complexity of the genetic code is millions of times greater than man's present technology, we can conclude that the originator of the information must be supremely intelligent.

Two biologist have noted,

DNA is an information code .... The overwhelming conclusion is that information does not and cannot arise spontaneously by mechanistic processes. Intelligence is a necessity in the origin of any informational code, including the genetic code, no matter how much time is given.[17]

God, in His Word, tells us that His creation is a witness to Himself and that we do not have an excuse for not believing (Romans 1:19–20). The fact that the information encoded in

---

[15] Gitt, W., *In the Beginning Was Information*, p. 107, 1997.

[16] Spetner, L., *Not by Chance*, p. 160, 1997.

[17] Lester, L., and Bohlin, R., *The Natural Limits to Biological Change*, p. 157, 1989.

DNA ultimately needs to have come from an infinite source of information testifies to a Creator. And, as we saw above, the only known way to link together left-handed amino acids is through purposeful design. Since no human was present to assemble the first living cell, it is further testimony to an all-wise Creator God.

GIVEN ENOUGH TIME ...

Nobel prize–winning scientist George Wald once wrote,

> However improbable we regard this event [evolution], or any of the steps it involves, given enough time, it will almost certainly happen at least once ... . Time is the hero of the plot ... . Given so much time, the impossible becomes possible, the possible becomes probable, the probable becomes virtually certain. One only has to wait; time itself performs miracles.[18]

[18]   Wald, G., The origin of life, *Scientific American* **191**:45, August 1954.

In the case of protein formation, the statement "given enough time" is not valid. When we look at the mathematical probabilities of even a small protein (100 amino acids) assembling by random chance, it is beyond anything that has ever been observed.

What is the probability of ever getting one small protein of 100 left-handed amino acids? (An average protein has at least 300 amino acids in it—all left-handed.) To assemble just 100 left-handed amino acids (far shorter than the average protein) would be the same probability as getting 100 heads in a row when flipping a coin. In order to get 100 heads in a row, we would have to flip a coin 10^{30} times (this is 10x10, 30 times). This is such an astounding improbability that there would not be enough time in the whole history of the universe (even according to evolutionary timeframes) for this to happen.

The ability of complex structures to form by naturalistic processes is essential for the evolution model to work. However, the complexity of life appears to preclude this from happening. According to the laws of probability, if the chance of an event occurring is smaller than 1 in 10^{-50}, then the event will never occur (this is equal to 1 divided by 10^{50} and is a very small number).[19]

What have scientists calculated the probability to be of an average-size protein occurring naturally? Walter Bradley, Ph.D. materials science, and Charles Thaxton, Ph.D. chemistry,[20] calculated that the probability of amino acids forming into a protein is

$$4.9 \times 10^{-191}.$$

This is well beyond the laws of probability (1×10^{-50}), and a

[19] Probability expert Emile Borel wrote, "Events whose probabilities are extremely small never occur .... We may be led to set at 1 to the 50th power the value of negligible probabilities on the cosmic scale." (Borel, E., *Probabilities and Life*, p. 28, 1962).

[20] Ref. 5.

protein is not even close to becoming a complete living cell. Sir Fred Hoyle, Ph.D. astronomy, and Chandra Wickramasinghe, Professor of Applied Math and Astronomy, calculated that the probability of getting a cell by naturalistic processes is

$$1 \times 10^{-40,000}.$$

> No matter how large the environment one considers, life cannot have had a random beginning .... There are about two thousand enzymes, and the chance of obtaining them all in a random trial is only one part in $(10^{20})^{2000} = 10^{40,000}$, an outrageously small probability that could not be faced even if the whole universe consisted of organic soup.[21]

CONCLUSION

As we have seen, the scientific evidence confirms that "in the beginning, God created ... ." Life cannot come from nonlife; only God can create life. True science and the Bible will always agree. Whether in biology, astronomy, geology or any other field of study, we can trust God's Word to be accurate when it speaks about these topics. Let us stand up for the truth of Genesis and take back our culture.

---

[21] Hoyle, F., and Wickramasinghe, C., *Evolution from Space*, p. 176, 1984.

ARE MUTATIONS PART OF THE "ENGINE" OF EVOLUTION?

BODIE HODGE

The box-office hits *X-Men* and its sequels are squarely based on the theory of evolution. In these movies (and in the comic books that inspired them), mutations are the driving force of the continuing evolution of humans. The very first lines of *X-Men* are, "Mutation: it is the key to our evolution. It has enabled us to evolve from a single-celled organism into the dominant species on the planet. This process is slow, normally taking thousands and thousands of years. But every few hundred millennia, evolution leaps forward." Are mutations really the "key to our evolution"? Do mutations provide the fuel for the engine of evolution? In this chapter, we take a close look at mutations to see what they are and what they are *not*. When we understand genetics and the limits of biological change, we will see how science confirms what the Bible says, "God made the beasts of the earth after their kind" (Genesis 1:25).

IN THE EVOLUTIONARY MODEL, MUTATIONS are hailed as a dominant mechanism for pond-scum-to-people evolution and provide "proof" that the Bible's history about creation is wrong. But are we to trust the ideas of imperfect, fallible men about how we came into existence, or should we believe the account of a perfect God who was an eyewitness to His creation? Let's look at mutations in more detail and see if they provide the information necessary to support pond-scum-to-people evolution, or if they confirm God's Word in Genesis.

Mutations are primarily permanent changes in the DNA strand. DNA (deoxyribonucleic acid) is the information storage unit for all organisms, including humans, cats and dogs. In humans, the DNA consists of about 3 billion base pairs. The DNA is made of two strands and forms a double helix. In sexual reproduction, one set of chromosomes (large segments of DNA) comes from the mother and one set from the father. In asexual reproduction, the DNA is copied whole and then passed along when the organism splits.

The double helix is made up of four types of nitrogen bases called *nucleotides*. These types are guanine, cytosine, adenine and thymine. They are represented by the letters G, C, A and T. Each

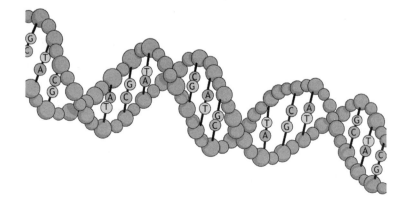

of these base pairs, or "letters," is part of a code that stores information for hair color, height, eye shape, etc. The bases pair up as follows: adenine to thymine and guanine to cytosine.

Think of it like Morse code. Morse code is a system in which letters are represented by dashes and dots (if audible, then it is a long sound and short sound). When you combine different dots and dashes, you can spell out letters and words. Here is a copy of Morse code:

A •–	N –•	0 ‑‑‑‑‑‑
B –•••	O ‑‑‑	1 •‑‑‑‑
C –•–•	P •‑‑•	2 ••‑‑‑
D –••	Q ‑‑•‑	3 •••‑‑
E •	R •–•	4 ••••‑
F ••–•	S •••	5 •••••
G ‑‑•	T –	6 –••••
H ••••	U ••–	7 ‑‑•••
I ••	V •••–	8 ‑‑‑••
J •‑‑‑	W •‑‑	9 ‑‑‑‑•
K –•–	X –••–	Fullstop •–•–•–
L •–••	Y –•‑‑	Comma ‑‑••‑‑
M ‑‑	Z ‑‑••	Query ••‑‑••

If someone wanted to call for help using Morse code, for instance, they would send the letters SOS (which is the international distress signal for *help*). Morse code for SOS is:

S is *dot dot dot* [• • •] or three short sounds.
O is *dash dash dash* [– – –] or three long sounds.
S is *dot dot dot* [• • •] or three short sounds.

Therefore, it would be [• • • – – – • • •] or three short sounds followed by three long sounds then followed by three short sounds again.

A mutation would be like changing a dot to a dash in Morse code. If we tried to spell SOS in Morse code, and changed the first dot to a dash, it would accidentally read:

[– • • – – – • • •]

Dash dot dot is the sequence for D, not S; so it would now read:

D [– • •]
O [– – –]
S [• • •]

So, because of the mistake (mutation), we now read DOS, instead of SOS. If you sent this, no one would think you needed help. This mutation was significant because it did two things to your message:

1. The original word was lost.

2. The intent/meaning was lost.

The DNA strand is similar to, but much more complicated than, Morse code. It uses four letters (G, A, T, C) instead of dashes and dots to make words and phrases. And like Morse code, mutations can affect the DNA strand and cause problems for the organism. These DNA mistakes are called *genetic* mutations.

Theoretically, genetic mutations (that are not static) can cause one of two things:

1. Loss of information[1]

2. Gain of new information

Virtually all observed mutations are in the category of *loss of*

---

[1]   For a definition of information that is based on the laws of science, see Gitt, W., *In the Beginning was Information*, CLV, Bielefeld, Germany, 1997.

information. This is different from loss or gain of *function.* Some mutations can cause an organism to lose genetic information and yet attain a beneficial outcome. This is rare but has happened. These types of mutations are often called *beneficial* mutations. For example, if a beetle loses the information to make a wing on a windy island, the mutation is beneficial because the beetle doesn't get blown out to sea and killed. Genetically, the mutation caused a loss of information but was helpful to the beetle. Thus, it was a beneficial mutation.

Besides mutations that cause information loss, in theory there could also be mutations that cause a *gain of new information.* There are only a few alleged cases of such mutations. However, if a mutated DNA strand were built up with a group of base pairs that didn't do anything, this strand wouldn't be useful. Therefore, to be useful to an organism, a mutation that has a gain of new information must also cause a gain of new function.

TYPES OF GENETIC MUTATIONS

The DNA strand contains instructions on how to make proteins. Every three "letters" code for a specific amino acid, such as TGC, ATC, GAT, TAG and CTC. Many amino acids together compose a protein. For simplicity's sake, to illustrate concepts with the DNA strand, we will use examples in English. Here is a segment illustrating DNA in three-letter words:

> The car was red. The red car had one key.
> The key has one eye and one tip.

POINT MUTATIONS

Point mutations are mutations where one letter changes on the DNA sequence. A point mutation in our example could cause "car" in the second sentence to be read "cat":

The car was red. The red **cat** had one key.
The key has one eye and one tip.

With this point mutation, we lost the information for one word (car) as well as changed the meaning of the sentence. We did gain one word (cat), but we lost one word (car) and lost the meaning of one phrase. So the overall result was a loss of information.

But many times, point mutations won't produce another word. Take for instance another point mutation, which changes "car" not to "cat" but to "caa":

The car was red. The red **caa** had one key.
The key has one eye and one tip.

With this point mutation, we lost the information for one word (car) as well as the meaning. We did not gain any new words, and we lost one word and lost the meaning of one phrase. So again, the overall result of this point mutation was a loss of information, but even more so this time.

Point mutations can be very devastating. There is a children's disease called Hutchinson-Gilford progeria syndrome (HGPS) or simply progeria. It was recently linked to a single point mutation. It is a mutation that causes children's skin to age, their head to go bald at a very early age (pre-kindergarten), their bones to develop problems usually associated with the elderly and their body size to remain very short (about one-half to two-thirds of normal height). Their body parts, including organs, age rapidly, which usually causes death at the average age of 13 years.[2]

Not all point mutations are as devastating, yet they still result

---

[2]   Hodge, B., One tiny flaw and 50 years lost, *Creation* **27**(1):33, 2004.

in a loss of information. According to biophysicist Lee Spetner, "All point mutations that have been studied on the molecular level turn out to reduce the genetic information and not to increase it."[3]

INVERSION MUTATIONS

An inversion mutation is a strand of DNA in a particular segment that reverses itself.

An inversion mutation would be like taking the second sentence of our example and spelling it backwards:

The car was red. Yek eno dah rac der eht.
The key has one eye and one tip.

With inversion mutations, we can lose quite a bit of information. We lost several words from, and the meaning of, the second sentence. These mutations can cause serious problems to the organism. The bleeding disorder hemophilia A is caused by an inversion in the Factor VIII (F8) gene.

INSERTION MUTATIONS

An insertion mutation is a segment of DNA, whether a single base pair or an extensive length, that is inserted into the DNA strand.

For this example, let's copy a word from the second sentence and insert it into the third sentence:

The car was red. The red car had one key.
Had the key has one eye and one tip.

This insertion really didn't help anything. In fact, the insertion is detrimental to the third sentence in that it makes the third sentence meaningless. So this copied word in the third

3 Spetner, L., *Not by Chance*, p. 138, 1997.

sentence destroyed the combined meanings of the eight words in the third sentence. Insertions generally result in a protein that loses function.[4]

DELETION MUTATIONS

A deletion mutation is a segment of DNA, whether a single base pair or an extensive length, that is deleted from the strand. This will be an obvious loss.

In this instance, the second sentence will be deleted.

The car was red. The key has one eye and one tip.

The entire second sentence has been lost. Thus, we have lost its meaning as well as the words that were in the sentence. Some disorders from deletion mutations are facioscapulohumeral muscular dystrophy (FSHD) and spinal muscular atrophy.[5]

FRAME SHIFT MUTATIONS

There are two basic types of frame shift mutations: frame shift due to an insertion and frame shift due to a deletion. These mutations can be caused by an insertion or deletion of one or more letters not divisible by three, which causes an offset in the reading of the "letters" of the DNA.

If a mutation occurs where one or more letters are inserted, then the entire sentence can be off. If a **t** were inserted at the beginning of the second sentence, it would read like this:

The car was red. T_t_h **ere** dca rha **don eke** yth **eke** yha **son** eey ean **don** eti p.

4 DNA Direct website, www.dnadirect.com/resource/genetics_101/GH_DNA_mutations.jsp.
5 Athena Diagnostics website, www.athenadiagnostics.com/site/content/diagnostic_ed/genetics_primer/part_2.asp.

Four new words were produced (two of them twice): *ere, don, eke* and *son*. These four words were not part of the original phrase. However, we lost 14 words. Not only did we lose these words, but we also lost the meaning behind the words. We lost 14 words while gaining only four new ones.

Therefore, even though the DNA strand became longer and produced four words via a single insertion, it lost fourteen other words. The overall effect was a loss of information.

A frame shift mutation can also occur by the deletion of one or more "letters." If the first **t** in the second sentence is deleted, the letters shift to the left, and we get:

The car was red. **Her** edc arh **ado** nek eyt hek
eyh aso **nee yea** ndo **net** ip.

Five new words were produced: *her, ado, nee, yea* and *net*. However, once again, we lost fourteen words. So again, the overall effect was a loss of information, and the DNA strand became smaller due to this mutation.

Frame shift mutations are usually detrimental to the organism by causing the resulting protein to be nonfunctional.

This is just the basics of mutations at a genetic level.[6]

WHAT DOES EVOLUTION TEACH ABOUT MUTATIONS?

Pond-scum-to-people evolution teaches that, over time, by natural causes, nonliving chemicals gave rise to a living cell. Then, this single-celled life form gave rise to more advanced life forms. In essence, over millions of years, increases in information caused by mutations plus natural selection developed all the life forms we see on Earth today.

---

[6]   For more on specific mutations and more complex examples, please visit www.AnswersInGenesis.org/mutations.

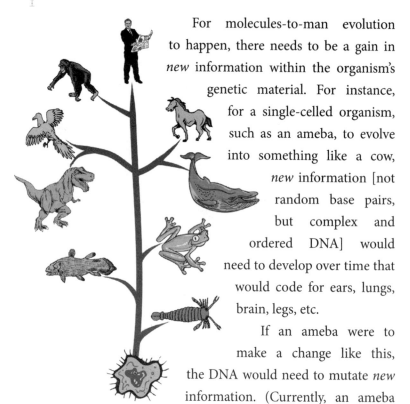

For molecules-to-man evolution to happen, there needs to be a gain in *new* information within the organism's genetic material. For instance, for a single-celled organism, such as an ameba, to evolve into something like a cow, *new* information [not random base pairs, but complex and ordered DNA] would need to develop over time that would code for ears, lungs, brain, legs, etc.

If an ameba were to make a change like this, the DNA would need to mutate *new* information. (Currently, an ameba has limited genetic information, such as the information for protoplasm.) This increase of new information would need to continue in order for a heart, kidneys, etc. to develop. If a DNA strand gets larger due to a mutation, but the sequence doesn't code for anything (e.g., it doesn't contain information for working lungs, heart, etc.), then the amount of DNA added is useless and would be more of a hindrance than a help.

There have been a few arguable cases of information-gaining mutations, but for evolution to be true, there would need to be *billions* of them. The fact is, we don't observe this in nature, but rather we see the opposite—organisms losing information. Organisms are changing, but the change is in the wrong direction! How can losses of information add up to a gain?

WHAT DOES THE BIBLE TEACH?

From a biblical perspective, we know that Adam and Eve had perfect DNA because God declared all that He had made "very good" (Genesis 1:31). This goes for the original animal and plant kinds as well. They originally had perfect DNA strands with no mistakes or mutations.

Genesis	Exodus	Leviticus
"Very good" Genesis 1:31		

ADAM & EVE

However, when man sinned against God (Genesis 3), God cursed the ground and the animals, and He sentenced man to die (Genesis 2:17; 3:19). In a sense, God withdrew some of His sustaining power to no longer uphold everything perfectly by His awesome power.

Since then, we would expect mutations to occur and DNA flaws to accumulate. The incredible amount of information that was originally in the DNA has been filtered out, and in many

Genesis	Exodus	Leviticus
SIN AND THE CURSE		

ADAM & EVE

Genesis 3

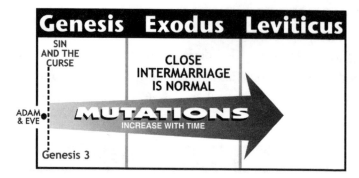

cases lost, due to mutations and natural selection.

At the time of Noah's Flood, there was a genetic bottleneck where information was lost among many land animals and humans. The only genetic information that survived came from the representatives of the kinds of land-dwelling, air-breathing animals and humans that were on the Ark.

Over time, as people increased on the earth, God knew that mutations were rising within the human population and declared that people should no longer intermarry with close relatives (Leviticus 18). Why did He do this? Intermarriage with close relatives results in the possibility of similar genetic mutations appearing in a child due to inheriting a common mutation from both the father and mother. If both parents inherited the same mutated gene from a common ancestor (e.g., a grandparent), this would increase the possibility of both parents passing this mutated gene

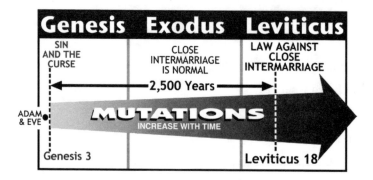

along to their child.

Marrying someone who is not a close relative reduces the chances that both would have the same mutated gene. If the segment of DNA from the mother had a mutation, it would be masked by the father's unmutated gene. If the segment of DNA from the father had a mutation, it would be masked by the mother's unmutated gene. If the genes from both parents were mutated, then the mutation would show in the child.[7] Our all-knowing God obviously knew this would happen and gave the command in Leviticus not to marry close relations.

<u>CONCLUSION</u>

The biblical perspective on change within living things doesn't require that new information be added to the genome as pond-scum-to-people evolution does. In fact, we expect to see the opposite (loss of genetic information) due to the Curse in Genesis 3. Biblically, we would expect mutations to produce defects in the genome and would not expect mutations to be adding much, if any, new information.

Observations confirm that mutations overwhelmingly cause a loss of information, not a net gain, as evolution requires.

Mutations, when properly understood, are an excellent example of science confirming the Bible. When one sees the devastating effects of mutations, one can't help but be reminded of the Curse in Genesis 3. The accumulation of mutations from generation to generation is due to man's sin. But those who have placed their faith in Christ, our Creator, look forward to a new heaven and Earth where there will be no more pain, death or disease.

---

[7] This is only true for recessive mutations like the one that causes cystic fibrosis. There are some dominant mutations that will appear in the child regardless of having a normal copy of the gene from one parent.

DID HUMANS REALLY EVOLVE FROM APELIKE CREATURES?

DR. DAVID MENTON

Television documentaries on human evolution abound. Some of the more popular in recent years have been *Walking with Cavemen* (2003) produced by BBC and aired on the Discovery Channel, *The Journey of Man: A Genetic Odyssey* (2003), produced by National Geographic and *Survivor: The Mystery of Us* (2005), also by National Geographic. All of these shows present as fact the story of human evolution from apelike creatures over the past several million years. They claim that anthropologists have found links in the human evolutionary chain and that scientists have "proven" evolution happens through DNA and other studies. But what is the real evidence for human evolution? What evidence are we not hearing? In this chapter, we will examine how anthropologists either make a man out of a monkey or make monkeys out of men. And once again, we'll conclude that the evidence points to the fact that man is a unique creation, made in the image of God.

PERHAPS THE MOST BITTER PILL to swallow for any
Christian who attempts to "make peace" with Darwin
is the presumed ape ancestry of man. Even many Christians who
uncritically accept evolution as "God's way of creating" try to
somehow elevate the origin of man, or at least his soul, above that
of the beasts. Evolutionists attempt to soften the blow by assuring
us that man didn't exactly evolve from apes (tailless monkeys) but
rather from *apelike* creatures. This is mere semantics, however,
as many of the presumed apelike ancestors of man are apes and
have scientific names, which include the word *pithecus* (derived
from the Greek meaning "ape"). The much-touted "human ancestor" commonly known as "Lucy," for example, has the scientific
name *Australopithecus afarensis* (meaning "southern *ape* from
the Afar triangle of Ethiopia"). But what does the Bible say about
the origin of man, and what exactly is the scientific evidence that
evolutionists claim for our ape ancestry?

BIBLICAL STARTING ASSUMPTIONS

God tells us that on the same day He made all animals that
walk on the earth (the sixth day), He created man separately in
His own image with the intent that man would have dominion
over every other living thing on Earth (Genesis 1:26–28). From
this it is clear that there is no animal that is man's equal, and certainly none his ancestor.

Thus when God paraded the animals by Adam for him to
name, He observed that "for Adam there was not found an help
meet for him" (Genesis 2:20). Jesus confirmed this uniqueness
of men and women when He declared that marriage is to be
between a man and a woman because "from the beginning of
the creation God made them male and female" (Mark 10:6).
This leaves no room for prehumans or for billions of years of

cosmic evolution prior to man's appearance on the earth. Adam chose the very name "Eve" for his wife because he recognized that she would be "the mother of all living" (Genesis 3:20). The Apostle Paul stated clearly that man is not an animal: "All flesh is not the same flesh: but there is one kind of flesh of men, another flesh of beasts, another of fishes, and another of birds" (1 Corinthians 15:39).

EVOLUTIONARY STARTING ASSUMPTIONS

While Bible-believing Christians begin with the assumption that God's Word is true and that man's ancestry goes back only to a fully human Adam and Eve, evolutionists begin with the assumption that man has, in fact, evolved from apes. No paleoanthropologists (those who study the fossil evidence for man's origin) would dare to seriously raise the question, "*Did* man evolve from apes?" The only permissible question is "From *which* apes did man evolve?"

Since evolutionists generally do not believe that man evolved from any ape that is now living, they look to fossils of humans and apes to provide them with their desired evidence. Specifically, they look for any anatomical feature that looks "intermediate" (between that of apes and man). Fossil apes having such features are declared to be ancestral to man (or at least collateral relatives) and are called *hominids*. Living apes, on the other hand, are not considered to be hominids, but rather are called *hominoids* because they are only similar to humans but did not evolve into them. Nonetheless, evolutionists are willing to accept mere similarities between the fossilized bones of extinct apes and the bones of living men as "proof" of our ape ancestry.

WHAT IS THE EVIDENCE FOR HUMAN EVOLUTION?

Though many similarities may be cited between living apes and humans, the only historical evidence that could support the ape ancestry of man must come from fossils. Unfortunately, the fossil record of man and apes is very sparse. Approximately 95% of all known fossils are marine invertebrates, about 4.7% are algae and plants, about 0.2% are insects and other invertebrates and only about 0.1% are vertebrates (animals with bones). Finally, only the smallest imaginable fraction of vertebrate fossils consists of primates (humans, apes, monkeys and lemurs).

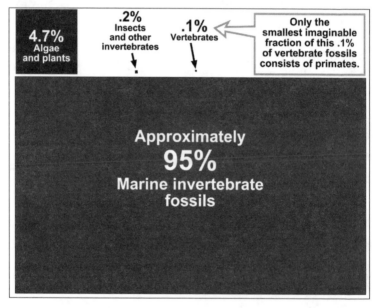

Because of the rarity of fossil hominids, even many of those who specialize in the evolution of man have never actually seen an original hominid fossil, and far fewer have ever had the opportunity to handle or study one. Most scientific papers on human evolution are based on casts of original specimens (or even on published photos, measurements and descriptions of them). Access to original fossil hominids is strictly limited by those who

discovered them and is often confined to a few favored evolutionists who agree with the discoverers' interpretation of the fossil.

Since there is much more prestige in finding an ancestor of
man than an ancestor of living apes (or worse yet, merely an extinct
ape), there is immense pressure on paleoanthropologists to declare
almost any ape fossil to be a "hominid." As a result, the living apes
have pretty much been left to find their own ancestors.

Many students in our schools are taught human evolution
(often in the social studies class!) by teachers having little knowledge of human anatomy, to say nothing of ape anatomy. But it is
useless to consider the fossil evidence for the evolution of man
from apes without first understanding the basic anatomical and
functional differences between human and ape skeletons.

JAWS AND TEETH

Because of their relative hardness, teeth and jaw fragments
are the most frequently found primate fossils. Thus, much of the
evidence for the ape ancestry of man is based on similarities of
teeth and jaws.

In contrast to man, apes tend to have incisor and canine teeth
that are relatively larger than their molars. Ape teeth usually have
thin enamel (the hardest surface layer of the tooth), while humans
generally have thicker enamel. Finally, the jaws tend to be more
U-shaped in apes and more parabolic in man.

The problem in declaring a fossil ape to be a human ancestor (i.e., a hominid) on the basis of certain humanlike features of
the teeth is that some living apes have these same features and
they are not considered to be ancestors of man. Some species of
modern baboons, for example, have relatively small canines and
incisors and relatively large molars. While most apes do have thin
enamel, some apes such as the orangutans have relatively thick

enamel. Clearly, teeth tell us more about an animal's diet and feeding habits than its supposed evolution. Nonetheless, thick enamel is one of the most commonly cited criteria for declaring an ape fossil to be a hominid.

Artistic imagination has been used to illustrate entire "apemen" from nothing more than a single tooth. In the early 1920s, the "apeman" *Hesperopithecus* (which consisted of a single

tooth) was pictured in the *London Illustrated News* complete with the tooth's wife, children, domestic animals and cave! Experts used this tooth, known as "Nebraska man," as proof for human evolution during the Scopes trial in 1925. In 1927 parts of the skeleton were discovered together with the teeth, and Nebraska man was found to really be an extinct peccary (wild pig)!

SKULLS

Skulls are perhaps the most interesting primate fossils because they house the brain and give us an opportunity, with the help of imaginative artists, to look our presumed ancestors in the face. The human skull is easily distinguished from all living apes, though there are, of course, similarities.

The vault of the skull is large in humans because of their relatively large brain compared to apes. Even so, the size of the normal adult human brain varies over nearly a threefold range.

These differences in size in the human brain do not correlate with intelligence. Adult apes have brains that are generally smaller than even the smallest of adult human brains and, of course, are

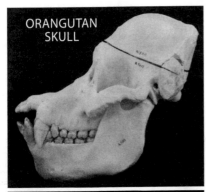

ORANGUTAN SKULL

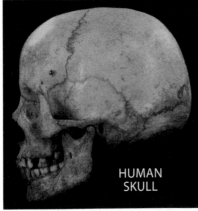

HUMAN SKULL

not even remotely comparable in intelligence.

Perhaps the best way to distinguish an ape skull from a human skull is to examine it from a side view. From this perspective, the face of the human is nearly vertical, while that of the ape slopes forward from its upper face to its chin.

From a side view, the bony socket of the eye (the orbit) of an ape is obscured by its broad flat upper face. Humans, on the other hand, have a more curved upper face and forehead, clearly revealing the orbit of the

eye from a side view.

Another distinctive feature of the human skull is the nose bones that our glasses rest on. Apes do not have protruding nasal bones and would have great difficulty wearing glasses.

LEG BONES

The most eagerly sought-after evidence in fossil hominids is any anatomical feature that might suggest *bipedality* (the ability to walk on two legs). Since humans walk on two legs, any evidence of bipedality in fossil apes is considered by evolutionists to be compelling evidence for human ancestry. But we should bear in mind that the way an ape walks on two legs is entirely different from the way man walks on two legs. The distinctive human gait requires the complex integration of many skeletal and muscular features in our hips, legs and feet. Thus, evolutionists closely examine the hipbones (*pelvis*), thighbones (*femur*), leg bones (*tibia* and *fibula*) and foot bones of fossil apes in an effort to detect any anatomical features that might suggest bipedality.

Evolutionists are particularly interested in the angle at which the femur and the tibia meet at the knee (called the *carrying angle*). Humans are able to keep their weight over their feet while walking because their femurs converge toward the knees, forming a carrying angle of approximately 9 degrees with the tibia (in other words, we're sort of knock-kneed). In contrast, chimps and gorillas have widely separated straight legs with a carrying angle of essentially 0 degrees. These animals manage to keep their weight over their feet when walking by swinging their body from side to side in the familiar "ape walk."

Evolutionists assume that fossil apes with a high carrying angle (humanlike) were bipedal and thus evolving into man. Certain australopithecines (an apelike creature) are considered to have walked like us and thus to be our ancestors largely because they had a high carrying angle. But high carrying angles are not confined to humans—they are also found on some modern apes that walk gracefully on tree limbs and only clumsily on the ground.

Living apes with a high carrying angle (values comparable to man) include such apes as the orangutan and spider monkey—both adept tree climbers and capable of only an apelike bipedal gait on the ground. The point is that there are *living* tree-dwelling apes and monkeys with some of the same anatomical features that evolutionists consider to be definitive evidence for bipedality, yet none of these animals walks like man and no one suggests they are our ancestors or descendants.

FOOT BONES

The human foot is unique and not even close to the appearance or function of the ape foot. The big toe of the human foot is inline with the foot and does not jut out to the side like apes. Human toe bones are relatively straight rather than curved and grasping like ape toes.

While walking, the heel of the human foot first hits the ground, then the weight distribution spreads from the heel along the outer margin of the foot up to the base of the little toe. From the little toe it spreads inward across the base of the toes and finally pushes off from the big toe. No ape has a foot or push-off like that of a human; and thus, no ape is capable of walking with our distinctive human stride, or of making human footprints.

HIPBONES

The pelvis (hipbones) plays a critically important role in walking, and the characteristic human gait requires a pelvis that is distinctly different from that of the apes. Indeed, one only has to examine the pelvis to determine if an ape has the ability to walk like a man.

The part of the hipbones that we can feel just under our belt is called the iliac blade. Viewed from above, these blades are curved forward like the handles of a steering yolk on an airplane. The iliac blades of the ape, in contrast, project straight out to the side like the handlebars of a scooter. It is simply not possible to walk like a human with an apelike pelvis. On this feature alone one can easily distinguish apes from humans.

ONLY THREE WAYS TO MAKE AN "APEMAN"

Knowing from Scripture that God didn't create any apemen, there are only three ways for the evolutionist to create one.

1   Combine ape fossil bones with human fossil bones and declare the two to be one individual—a real "apeman."

2   Emphasize certain humanlike qualities of fossilized ape bones, and with imagination upgrade apes to be more humanlike.

3   Emphasize certain apelike qualities of fossilized human bones, and with imagination downgrade humans to be more apelike.

These three approaches account for *all* of the attempts by evolutionists to fill the unbridgeable gap between apes and men with fossil apemen.

COMBINING MEN AND APES

The most famous example of an apeman proven to be a combination of ape and human bones is Piltdown man. In 1912,

Charles Dawson, a medical doctor and an amateur paleontologist, discovered a mandible (lower jawbone) and part of a skull in a gravel pit near Piltdown, England. The jawbone was apelike but had teeth that showed wear similar to the human pattern. The skull, on the other hand, was very humanlike. These two specimens were combined to form what was called "Dawn man," which was calculated to be 500,000 years old.

The whole thing turned out to be an elaborate hoax. The skull was indeed human (about 500 years old), while the jaw was that of a modern female orangutan whose teeth had been obviously filed to crudely resemble the human wear pattern. Indeed, the long ape canine tooth was filed down so far that it exposed the pulp chamber, which was then filled in to hide the mischief. It would seem that any competent scientist examining this tooth would have concluded that it was either a hoax or the world's first root canal! The success of this hoax for over 50 years, in spite of the careful scrutiny of the best authorities in the world, led the human evolutionist Sir Solly Zuckerman to declare: "It is doubtful if there is any science at all in the search for man's fossil ancestry."[1]

MAKING MAN OUT OF APES

Many apemen are merely apes that evolutionists have attempted to upscale to fill the gap between apes and men. These include all the australopithecines, as well as a host of other extinct apes such as *Ardipithecus*, *Orrorin*, *Sahelanthropus* and *Kenyanthropus*. All have obviously ape skulls, ape pelvises and ape hands and feet. Nevertheless, australopithecines (especially *Australopithecus afarensis*) are often portrayed as having hands and feet identical to modern man, a ramrod-straight, upright posture and

---

[1] Zuckerman, S., *Beyond the Ivory Tower*, p. 64, 1970.

a human gait.

The best-known specimen of A. *afarensis* is the fossil commonly known as "Lucy." A life-like mannequin of "Lucy" in the *Living World* exhibit at the St. Louis Zoo shows a hairy humanlike female body with human hands and feet but with an obviously apelike head. The three-foot-tall Lucy stands erect in a deeply pensive pose with her right forefinger curled under her chin, her eyes gazing off into the distance as if she were contemplating the mind of Newton.

Few visitors are aware that this is a gross misrepresentation of what is known about the fossil ape *Australopithecus afarensis*. These apes are known to be long-armed knuckle-walkers with locking wrists. Both the hands and feet of this creature are clearly apelike. Paleoanthropologists Jack Stern and Randall Sussman[2] have reported that the hands of this species are "surprisingly similar to hands found in the small end of the pygmy chimpanzee–common chimpanzee range." They report that the feet, like the hands, are "long, curved and heavily muscled" much like those of living tree-dwelling primates. The authors conclude that no living primate has such hands and feet "for any purpose other than to meet the demands of full or part-time arboreal (tree-dwelling) life."

Despite evidence to the contrary, evolutionists and museums continue to portray Lucy (A. *Afarensis*) with virtually human feet (though some are finally showing the hands with long curved fingers).

MAKING APES OUT OF MAN

In an effort to fill the gap between apes and men, certain fossil *men* have been declared to be "apelike" and thus, ancestral

---

[2]   *American Journal of Physical Anthropology* **60**:279–317, 1983.

to at least "modern" man. You might say this latter effort seeks to make a "monkey" out of man. Human fossils that are claimed to be "apemen" are generally classified under the genus *Homo* (meaning "self"). These include *Homo erectus, Homo heidelbergensis* and *Homo neanderthalensis*.

The best-known human fossils are of Cro-Magnon man (whose marvelous paintings are found on the walls of caves in France) and Neandertal man. Both are clearly human and have long been classified as *Homo sapiens*. In recent years, however, Neandertal man has been downgraded to a different species— *Homo neanderthalensis*. The story of how Neandertal man was demoted to an apeman provides much insight into the methods of evolutionists.

Neandertal man was first discovered in 1856 by workmen digging in a limestone cave in the Neander valley near Dusseldorf, Germany. The fossil bones were examined by an anatomist (professor Schaafhausen) who concluded that they were human.

At first, not much attention was given to these finds, but with the publication of Darwin's *Origin of Species* in 1859, the search began for the imagined "apelike ancestors" of man. Darwinians argued that Neandertal man was an apelike creature, while many critical of Darwin (like the great anatomist Rudolph Virchow) argued that Neandertals were human in every respect, though some appeared to be suffering from rickets or arthritis.

Over 300 Neandertal specimens have now been found scattered throughout most of the world, including Belgium, China, Central and North Africa, Iraq, the Czech republic, Hungary, Greece, northwestern Europe and the Middle East. This race of men was characterized by prominent eyebrow ridges (like modern Australian Aborigines), a low forehead, a long narrow skull, a protruding upper jaw and a strong lower jaw with a short chin. They were deep-chested, large-boned individuals with a powerful build. It should be emphasized, however, that none of these features fall outside the range of normal human anatomy. Interestingly, the brain size (based on cranial capacity) of Neandertal man was actually *larger* than average for that of modern man, though this is rarely emphasized.

Most of the misconceptions about Neandertal man resulted from the claims of the Frenchman Marcelin Boule who, in 1908, studied two Neandertal skeletons that were found in France (LeMoustier and La Chapelle-aux-Saints). Boule declared Neandertal men to be anatomically and intellectually inferior brutes who were more closely related to apes than humans. He asserted that they had a slumped posture, a "monkey-like" arrangement of certain spinal vertebrae and even claimed that their feet were of a "grasping type" (like those of gorillas and chimpanzees). Boule concluded that Neandertal man could not have walked erectly, but rather must have walked in a clumsy fashion. These highly biased and inaccurate views prevailed and were even expanded by many other evolutionists up to the mid-1950s.

In 1957, the anatomists William Straus and A. J. Cave examined one of the French Neandertals (La Chapelle-aux-Saints) and determined that the individual suffered from severe arthritis (as suggested by Virchow nearly 100 years earlier), which had affected the vertebrae and bent the posture. The jaw also had been affected. These observations are consistent with the Ice Age climate in which Neandertals had lived. They may well have sought shelter in caves and this, together with poor diet and lack of sunlight, could easily have lead to diseases that affect the bones, such as rickets.

In addition to anatomical evidence, there is a growing body of cultural evidence for the fully human status of Neandertals. They buried their dead and had elaborate funeral customs that included arranging the body and covering it with flowers. They made a variety of stone tools and worked with skins and leather. A wood flute was recently discovered among Neandertal remains. There is even evidence that suggests that he engaged in medical care. Some Neandertal specimens show evidence of survival to old age despite numerous wounds, broken bones, blindness and disease. This suggests that these individuals were cared for and nurtured by others who showed human compassion.

Still, efforts continue to be made to somehow dehumanize Neandertal man. Many evolutionists now even insist that Neanderthal man is not even directly related to modern man because of some differences in a small fragment of DNA! There is, in fact, nothing about Neandertals that is in any way inferior to modern man. One of the world's foremost authorities on Neandertal man, Erik Trinkaus, concludes: "Detailed comparisons of Neanderthal skeletal remains with those of modern humans have shown that there is nothing in Neanderthal anatomy that conclusively indicates locomotor, manipulative, intellectual or linguistic abilities inferior to those of modern humans."[3]

CONCLUSION

Why then are there continued efforts to make apes out of man and man out of apes? In one of the most remarkably frank and candid assessments of the whole subject and methodology of paleoanthropology, Dr. David Pilbeam (a distinguished professor of anthropology) suggested the following:

> Perhaps generations of students of human evolution, including myself, have been flailing about in the dark; that our data base is too sparse, too

---

[3] *Natural History* **87**:10, 1978.

slippery, for it to be able to mold our theories. Rather the theories are more statements about us and ideology than about the past. Paleoanthropology reveals more about how humans view themselves than it does about how humans came about. But that is heresy.[4]

Oh, that these heretical words were printed as a warning on every textbook, magazine, newspaper article and statue that presumes to deal with the bestial origin of man!

No, we are not descended from apes. Rather, God created man as the crown of His creation on Day Six. We are a special creation of God, made in His image, to bring Him glory. What a revolution this truth would make, if our evolutionized culture truly understood it!

[4] *American Scientist* **66**:379, 1978.

Does the Bible Say anything about Astronomy?

Dr. Jason Lisle

The Bible is often attacked as a book that is scientifically out of date. Many television documentaries feature so-called "biblical scholars" who deride the Bible and tell us that it is a collection of myths and sayings compiled over thousands of years and that we can't trust the history or the science in the Bible. However, the Bible has been shown to be correct over and over again in matters of history and science. In this chapter we will see that, while not a science textbook, the Bible is accurate when it touches on astronomy; in fact, the Bible's teaching that the universe is only several thousand years old fits with our astronomical observations. We can trust the Word of the God who "gives the sun for light by day and the fixed order of the moon and the stars for light by night" (Jeremiah 31:35).

THE BIBLE IS THE HISTORY book of the universe. It tells us how the universe began and how it came to be the way it is today.

The Bible is much more than just a history book, however; it was written by inspiration of God. The Lord certainly understands how this universe works; after all, He made it. So His Word, the Bible, gives us the foundation for understanding the universe.

It has been said that the Bible is not a science textbook. This is true, of course, and it's actually a good thing. After all, our science textbooks are based on the ideas of human beings who do not know everything and who often make mistakes. That's why science textbooks change from time to time, as people discover new evidence and realize that they were wrong about certain things.

The Bible, though, never changes because it never needs to. God got it right the first time! The Bible is the infallible Word of God. So when it touches on a particular topic, it's right. When the Bible talks about geology, it's correct. When Scripture addresses biology or anthropology, it's also right.

What does the Bible teach about astronomy? Let's take a look at some of the things the Bible has to say about the universe. We will see that the Bible is absolutely correct when it deals with astronomy.

THE EARTH IS ROUND

The Bible indicates that the earth is round. One verse we can look at is Isaiah 40:22, where it mentions the "circle of the earth." From space, the earth always appears as a circle since it is round. This matches perfectly with the Bible.

Another verse to consider is

Job 26:10, where it teaches that God has "inscribed" a circle on the surface of the waters at the boundary of light and darkness. This boundary between light and darkness is where evening and morning occur. The boundary is a circle since the earth is round.

THE EARTH FLOATS IN SPACE

A very interesting verse to consider is Job 26:7, which states that God "hangs the earth on nothing." This might make you think of God hanging the earth like a Christmas tree ornament, but hanging it on empty space. Although this verse is written in a poetic way, it certainly seems to suggest that the earth floats in space; and indeed the earth does float in space. We now have pictures of the earth taken from space that show it floating in the cosmic void. The earth literally hangs upon nothing, just as the Bible suggests.

- The Hindus believed the earth to be supported on the backs of four elephants, which stand on the shell of a gigantic tortoise floating on the surface of the world's waters.

- The earth of the Vedic priests was set on 12 solid pillars; its upper side was its only habitable side.

- The Altaic people of Northern Siberia affirm that their mighty Ulgen created the earth on the waters and placed under it three great fish to support it.

- The Tartars and many of the other tribes of Eurasia believed the earth to be supported by a great bull.

THE EXPANSION OF THE UNIVERSE

The Bible indicates in several places that the universe has been "stretched out" or expanded. For example, Isaiah 40:22 teaches that God stretches out the heavens like a curtain and spreads them out like a tent to dwell in. This would suggest that the universe has actually increased in size since its creation. God is stretching it out, causing it to expand.

Now, this verse must have seemed very strange when it was first written. The universe certainly doesn't *look* as if it is expanding. After all, if you look at the night sky tonight, it will appear about the same size as it did the previous night, and the night before that.

In fact, secular scientists once believed that the universe was eternal and unchanging. The idea of an expanding universe would have been considered nonsense to most scientists of the past. So it must have been tempting for Christians to reject what the Bible teaches about the expansion of the universe.

I wonder if any Christians tried to "reinterpret" Isaiah 40:22 to read it in an unnatural way so that they wouldn't have to believe in an expanding universe. When the secular world believes one thing and the Bible teaches another, it is always tempting to think that God got the details wrong. But God is never wrong.

Most astronomers today believe that the universe is indeed expanding. In the 1920s, astronomers discovered that virtually all clusters of galaxies appear to be moving away from all other clusters; this indicates that the entire universe is expanding.

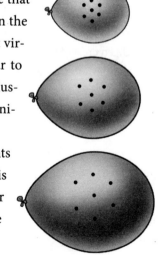

You can think of this like points on a balloon. As the balloon is inflated, all the points move farther away from each other. If the entire universe was being stretched out, the galaxies would all be moving away; and that is what they actually appear to be doing.

It is fascinating that the Bible recorded the idea of an expanding universe thousands of years before secular science came to accept the idea.

THE AGE OF THE UNIVERSE

Scripture also addresses the age of the universe. The Bible teaches that the entire universe was created in six days (Exodus 20:11). We know from the genealogies and other events recorded in Scripture that this creation happened about 6,000 years ago.

Yet, this is quite different from what most schools teach. Most secular scientists believe that the universe is many billions of years old and they usually hold to the big bang theory. The big bang is a secular speculation about the origin of the universe; it is an alternative to the Bible's teaching. The big bang attempts to explain the origin of the universe without God (see the next chapter, "Does the big bang fit with the Bible?").

People who believe in the big bang usually interpret the evidence according to their already-existing belief in the big bang. In other words, they just assume that the big bang is true; they interpret the evidence to match their beliefs. Of course, the Bible can also be used to interpret the evidence. And since the Bible records the true history of the universe, we see that it makes a lot more sense of the evidence than the big bang does.

Now let's look at some facts about the universe regarding its age. We will see that the evidence is consistent with 6,000 years but doesn't make sense if we hold to the big bang.

Of course, big bang supporters can always reinterpret the evidence by adding extra assumptions. So, the following facts are not intended to "prove" that the Bible is right about the age of the universe. The Bible is right in all matters because it is the Word of God. However, when we understand the scientific evidence, we will find that it agrees with what the Bible teaches. The evidence is certainly consistent with a young universe.

RECESSION OF THE MOON

The moon is slowly moving away from the earth. As the moon orbits the earth, its gravity pulls on the earth's oceans, which causes tides. The tides actually "pull forward" on the moon, causing the moon to gradually spiral outward. So the moon moves about an inch and a half away from the earth every year. That means that the moon would have been closer to the earth in the past.

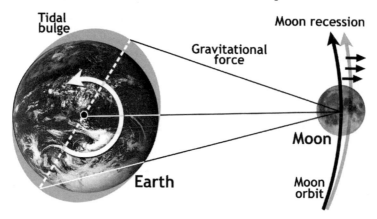

For example, six thousand years ago, the moon would have been about 800 feet closer to the earth (which is not much of a change, considering the moon is a quarter of a million miles away). So this "spiraling away" of the moon is not a problem over the biblical timescale of 6,000 years. But if the earth and moon were over four billion years old (as evolutionists teach), then we would have big problems. In this case, the moon would have been so close that it would actually have been touching the earth only 1.4 billion years ago. This problem suggests that the moon can't possibly be as old as secular astronomers claim.

Secular astronomers who assume that the big bang is true must use other explanations to get around this. For example, they might assume that the rate at which the moon was receding was actually smaller in the past. But this is an extra assumption needed to make their billions-of-years model work. The simplest explanation is that the moon hasn't been around for that long. The recession of the moon is a problem for a belief in billions of years but is perfectly consistent with a young age.

MAGNETIC FIELDS OF THE PLANETS

Many of the planets of the solar system have strong magnetic fields. These fields are caused by electrical currents that decay with time. We can even measure this decay of the earth's magnetic field: it gets weaker and weaker every year. If the planets were really billions of years old (as evolutionists believe) then their magnetic fields should be extremely weak by now. Yet they are not. The outer planets of the solar system, in particular, have quite strong magnetic fields. A reasonable explanation for this is that these planets are only a few thousand years old, as the Bible teaches.

SPIRAL GALAXIES

A galaxy is an enormous assembly of stars, interstellar gas and dust. The galaxy in which we live is called the Milky Way; it has over 100 billion stars. Some galaxies are round or elliptical. Others have an irregular shape, but some of the most beautiful galaxies are spiral in nature, such as our own. Spiral galaxies slowly rotate, but the inner regions of the spiral rotate faster than the outer regions. This means that a spiral galaxy is constantly becoming more and more twisted up as the spiral becomes tighter. After a few hundred million years, the galaxy would be wound so tightly that the spiral structure would no longer be recognizable.

According to the big bang scenario, galaxies are supposed to be many billions of years old. Yet we do see spiral galaxies—and lots of them. This suggests that they are not nearly as old as the big bang requires. Spiral galaxies are consistent with the biblical age of the universe but are problematic for a belief in billions of years.

NASA/STScI

COMETS

Comets are balls of ice and dirt. Many of them orbit the sun in elliptical paths. They spend most of their time far away from the sun, but occasionally they come very close to it. Every time a comet comes near the sun, some of its icy material is blasted away by the solar radiation. As a result, comets can orbit the sun for only so long (perhaps about 100,000 years at most) before they completely run out of material. Since we still have a lot of comets, this suggests that the solar system is much younger than 100,000 years; this agrees perfectly with the Bible's history.

Yet, secular astronomers believe the solar system is 4.5 billion years old. Since comets can't last that long, secular astronomers must assume that new comets are created to replace those that are gone. So they've invented the idea of an "Oort cloud." This is supposed to be a vast reservoir of icy masses orbiting far away from the sun. The idea is that occasionally an icy mass falls into the inner solar system to become a "new" comet. It is interesting that there is currently no evidence of an Oort cloud. And there's no reason to believe in one if we accept the creation account in Genesis. Comets are consistent with the fact that the solar system is young.

SUPERNATURAL CREATION

Aside from age, there are other indications that the universe was supernaturally created as the Bible teaches. These evidences show God's creativity—not a big bang. For example, astronomers have discovered "extrasolar" planets. These are planets that orbit distant stars—not our sun. These planets have not been directly observed. Instead, they have been detected indirectly—usually by the gravitational "tug" they produce on the star they orbit. But the principles being used here are all good "operational science"—the kind of testable, repeatable science that can be done in a laboratory. So we have every reason to believe that these are indeed real planets that God created.

These extrasolar planets are actually a problem for big-bang, evolutionary models of solar system formation. Secular astronomers had expected that other solar systems would resemble ours—with small planets forming very closely to their star and large planets (like Jupiter and Saturn) forming farther away. But many of these extrasolar planets are just the opposite; they are large Jupiter-sized planets orbiting very closely to their star. This is inconsistent with evolutionary models of solar system formation, but it's not a problem for biblical creation. God can create many different varieties of solar systems, and apparently He has done just that.

CONCLUSION

We have seen that when the Bible addresses the topic of astronomy, it is accurate in every aspect. This shouldn't be surprising because the Bible, which teaches that the heavens declare the glory and handiwork of God (Psalm 19:1), is the written Word of the Creator. God understands every aspect of the universe He has created, and He never makes mistakes.

In addition, the Word of God provides the correct foundation for understanding the scientific evidence. At the same time, the Bible provides more than just information on the physical universe. It also answers the most profound questions of life. Why are we here? How should we live? And what happens when we die? The Word of God even answers the question of why there is death and suffering in the world.[1]

We can have confidence that what the Bible says about our need for salvation is true, because the Bible has demonstrated itself to be accurate time after time. Showing our children how true science confirms the Bible will help them answer the evolutionary attacks they encounter at schools and in the media.

---

[1]   See www.AnswersInGenesis.org/curse.

DOES THE BIG BANG FIT WITH THE BIBLE?

DR. JASON LISLE

Astronomy has been much in the news these past several years as we see or read reports about the latest discoveries of the Hubble Space Telescope, the twin Mars' rovers *Spirit* and *Opportunity*, and the numerous space probes such as *Galileo*, *Cassini* and *Huygens*. All of these space programs assume that the universe began with a big bang billions of years ago. The public, for the most part, swallows these stories without any critical thinking. But is the big bang a truly scientific theory? Has "science" proven the age of the universe? In this chapter, we will explore the big bang and see why many scientists are abandoning the theory. We will see why the big bang doesn't fit the Bible or science.

THE "BIG BANG" IS A story about how the universe came into existence. It proposes that billions of years ago the universe began in a tiny, infinitely hot and dense point called a *singularity*. This singularity supposedly contained not only all the mass and energy that would become everything we see today, but also "space" itself. According to the story, the singularity rapidly expanded, spreading out the energy and space.

It is supposed that over vast periods of time, the energy from the big bang cooled down as the universe expanded. Some of it turned into matter—hydrogen and helium gas. These gases collapsed to form stars and galaxies of stars. Some of the stars created the heavier elements in their  core and then exploded, distributing these elements into space. Some of the heavier elements allegedly began to stick together and formed the earth and other planets.

This story of origins is entirely fiction. But sadly, many people claim to believe the big bang model. It is particularly distressing that many professing Christians have been taken in by the big bang, perhaps without realizing its atheistic underpinnings. They have chosen to reinterpret the plain teachings of Scripture in an attempt to make it mesh with secular beliefs about origins.

SECULAR COMPROMISES

There are several reasons why we cannot just add the big bang to the Bible. Ultimately, the big bang is a *secular* story of origins. When first proposed, it was an attempt to explain how the universe could have been created without God. Really, it is an *alternative* to the Bible; so it makes no sense to try to "add" it to the Bible. Let us examine some of the profound differences between the Bible and the secular big bang view of origins.

The Bible teaches that God created the universe in six days (Genesis 1; Exodus 20:11). It is clear from the context in Genesis that these were days in the ordinary sense (i.e., 24-hour days) since they are bounded by evening and morning and occur in an ordered list (second day, third day, etc.). Conversely, the big bang teaches the universe has evolved over billions of years.

The Bible says that Earth was created before the stars and that trees were created before the sun.[1] However, the big bang view teaches the exact opposite. The Bible tells us that the earth was

Big Bang	Stars	Sun	Molten Earth	First oceans
15 Billion years ago	10 Billion years ago	5 Billion years ago	4.5 Billion years ago	3.8 Billion years ago
Water covered Earth	Dry land and plants	Sun, moon and stars	Sea and flying creatures	Land animals and man
Day 1-2	Day 3	Day 4	Day 5	Day 6

---

[1] The sun and stars were made on Day 4 (Genesis 1:14–19). The earth was made on Day 1 (Genesis 1:1–5). Trees were made on Day 3 (Genesis 1:11–13).

created as a paradise; the secular model teaches it was created as a molten blob. The big bang and the Bible certainly do not agree about the past.

Many people don't realize that the big bang is a story not only about the past but also about the future. The most popular version of the big bang teaches that the universe will expand forever and eventually run out of usable energy. According to the story, it will remain that way forever in a state that astronomers call "heat death."[2] But the Bible teaches that the world will be judged and remade. Paradise will be restored. The big bang denies this crucial biblical teaching.

SCIENTIFIC PROBLEMS WITH THE BIG BANG

The big bang also has a number of scientific problems. Big bang supporters are forced to accept on "blind faith" a number of notions that are completely *inconsistent* with real observational

---

[2] Despite the name "heat death," the universe would actually be exceedingly cold.

science. Let's explore some of the inconsistencies between the big bang story and the real universe.

MISSING MONOPOLES

Most people know something about magnets—like the kind found in a compass or the kind that sticks to a refrigerator. We often say that magnets have two "poles"—a north pole and a south pole. Poles that are alike will repel each other, while opposites attract. A "monopole" is a hypothetical massive particle that is just like a magnet but has only one pole. So a monopole would have either a north pole or a south pole, but not both.

Particle physicists claim that many magnetic monopoles should have been created in the high temperature conditions of the big bang. Since monopoles are stable, they should have lasted to this day. Yet, despite considerable search efforts, monopoles have not been found. Where are the monopoles? The fact that we don't find any monopoles suggests that the universe never was that hot. This indicates that there never was a big bang, but it is perfectly consistent with the Bible's account of creation, since the universe did not start infinitely hot.

THE FLATNESS PROBLEM

Another serious challenge to the big bang model is called the "flatness problem." The expansion rate of the universe appears to be very finely balanced with the force of gravity; this condition is called "flat." If the universe were the accidental byproduct of a big bang, it is difficult to imagine how such a fantastic coincidence could occur. Big bang cosmology cannot explain why the matter density in the universe isn't greater, causing it to collapse upon itself (closed universe), or less, causing the universe to rapidly fly apart (open universe).

The problem is even more severe when we extrapolate into

the past. Since any deviation from perfect flatness tends to increase as time moves forward, it logically follows that the universe must have been *even more* precisely balanced in the past than it is today. Thus, at the moment of the big bang, the universe would have been

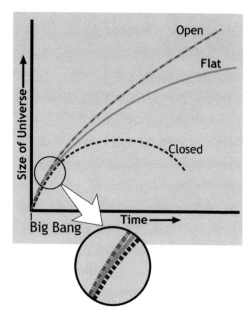

virtually flat to an extremely high precision. This must have been the case (assuming the big bang), despite the fact that the laws of physics allow for an *infinite* range of values. This is a coincidence that stretches credulity to the breaking point. Of course, in the creation model, "balance" is expected since the Lord has fine-tuned the universe for life.

INFLATING THE COMPLEXITIES

Many secular astronomers have come up with an idea called "inflation" in an attempt to address the flatness and monopole problems (as well as other problems not addressed in detail here, such as the horizon problem). Inflation proposes that the universe temporarily went through a period of accelerated expansion. Amazingly, there is no real supporting evidence for inflation; it appears to be nothing more than an unsubstantiated conjecture—much like the big bang itself. Moreover, the inflation idea has difficulties of its own, such as what would start it and how it would stop smoothly. In addition, other problems with the big bang are not solved, even if inflation were true. These are examined below.

WHERE IS THE ANTIMATTER?

Consider the "baryon number problem." Recall that the big bang supposes that matter (hydrogen and helium gas) was created from energy as the universe expanded. However, experimental physics tells us that whenever matter is created from energy, such a reaction also produces *antimatter*. Antimatter has similar properties to matter, except the charges of the particles are reversed. (So whereas a proton has a positive charge, an antiproton has a *negative* charge.) Any reaction where energy is transformed into matter produces an exactly equal amount of antimatter; there are no known exceptions.

The big bang (which has no matter to begin with—only energy) should have produced exactly equal amounts of matter and antimatter, and that should be what we see today. But we do not. The visible universe is comprised almost entirely of matter—with only trace amounts of antimatter anywhere.

This devastating problem for the big bang is actually consistent with biblical creation; it is a design feature. God created the universe to be essentially matter only—and it's a good thing He did. When matter and antimatter come together, they violently destroy each other. If the universe had equal amounts of matter and antimatter (as the big bang requires), life would not be possible.

MISSING POPULATION III STARS

The big bang model by itself can only account for the existence of the three lightest elements (hydrogen, helium and trace amounts of lithium). This leaves about 90 or so of the other naturally occurring elements to be explained. Since the conditions in the big bang are not right to form these heavier elements (as big bang supporters readily concede), secular astronomers believe that stars have produced the remaining elements by nuclear fusion in the core. This is thought to occur in the final stages of a massive star as it explodes (a supernova). The explosion then distributes the heavier elements into space. Second and third generation stars are thus "contaminated" with small amounts of these heavier elements.

If this story were true, then the *first* stars would have been comprised of only the three lightest elements (since these would have been the only elements in existence initially). Some such stars[3] should still be around today since their potential lifespan is calculated to exceed the (big bang) age of the universe. Such stars would be called "Population III" stars.[4] Amazingly (to those who believe in the big bang), Population III stars have not been found anywhere. All known stars have at least trace amounts of heavy elements in them. It is amazing to think that our galaxy alone is estimated to have over 100 billion stars in it. Yet not one star has been discovered that is comprised of *only* the three lightest elements.

THE COLLAPSE OF THE BIG BANG

With all the problems listed above, as well as many others too numerous to include, it is not surprising that quite a few secular astronomers are beginning to abandon the big bang. Although it is still the dominant model at present, increasing numbers of

---

[3] Small (red main sequence) stars do not use up their fuel quickly. These stars theoretically have enough fuel to last significantly longer than the estimated age of the (big bang) universe.

[4] If a star has a very small amount of heavy elements, it is called a "Population II" star. Pop. II stars exist primarily in the central bulge of spiral galaxies, in globular star clusters and in elliptical galaxies. If a star has a relatively large amount of heavy elements (like the sun) it is called "Population I." These stars exist primarily in the arms of spiral galaxies. The (hypothetical) Pop. III star would have no heavy elements at all.

physicists and astronomers are realizing that the big bang simply is not a good explanation of how the universe began. In the May 22, 2004 issue of *New Scientist*, there appeared an open letter to the scientific community written primarily by *secular* scientists[5] who challenge the big bang. These scientists pointed out that the copious arbitrary assumptions and the lack of successful big bang predictions challenge the legitimacy of the model. Among other things, they state:

> The big bang today relies on a growing number of hypothetical entities, things that we have never observed—inflation, dark matter and dark energy are the most prominent examples. Without them, there would be a fatal contradiction between the observations made by astronomers and the predictions of the big bang theory. In no other field of physics would this continual recourse to new hypothetical objects be accepted as a way of bridging the gap between theory and observation. It would, at the least, raise serious questions about the validity of the underlying theory.[6]

This statement has since been signed by hundreds of other scientists and professors at various institutions. The big bang seems to be losing considerable popularity. Secular scientists are increasingly rejecting the big bang, in favor of other models. If the big bang is abandoned, what will happen to all the Christians

---

[5] The alternatives to the big bang that these scientists had suggested are equally unbiblical. These included a steady-state theory and plasma cosmology.

[6] Lerner, E., *et al.*, An open letter to the scientific community, *New Scientist* **182**(2448):20, May 22, 2004. Available online at www.cosmologystatement.org.

who compromised and claimed that the Bible is compatible with the big bang? What will they say? Will they claim that the Bible actually does not teach the big bang, but instead that it teaches the latest secular model? Secular models come and go, but God's Word does not need to be changed because God got it exactly right the first time.

CONCLUSION

The big bang has many scientific problems. These problems are symptomatic of the underlying incorrect worldview. The big bang erroneously assumes that the universe was *not* supernaturally created, but that it came about by natural pro- cesses billions of years ago. However, reality does not line up with this notion. Biblical creation explains the evidence in a more straightforward way without the ubiquitous speculations prevalent in secular models. But ultimately, the best reason to reject the big bang is that it goes against what the Creator of the universe Himself has taught: "In the beginning, God created the heaven and the earth" (Genesis 1:1).

WHERE DID THE IDEA OF "MILLIONS OF YEARS" COME FROM?

DR. TERRY MORTENSON

All of our media outlets push evolution and "millions of years" ideas on the public. Even children's cartoons reflect evolutionary philosophy! In an episode of the cartoon *SpongeBob SquarePants*, entitled "SpongeBob B.C.," the narrator begins: "Ah, dawn breaks over the primordial sea. It is here that millions of years ago, life began taking its first clumsy steps out of the darkness, opening its newly formed eyeballs to stare into the blinding light of intelligence." Unfortunately, large segments of the church have swallowed the millions-of-years evolutionary history hook, line and sinker. But it was not always this way. In this chapter, we will discover where the idea of millions of years came from and why the church went along with it. We will see that science does not require it, but rather it is a necessity of uniformitarian geology and evolutionary theory.

TODAY, MOST PEOPLE IN THE world, including most people in the church, take for granted that the earth and universe are millions and millions (even billions) of years old. Our public schools, from kindergarten on up, teach these vast ages, and one is scoffed at if he questions them. But it has not always been that way, and it is important to understand how this change took place and why.

GEOLOGY'S EARLY BEGINNINGS

Geology as a separate field of science with systematic field studies, collection and classification of rocks and fossils, and development of theoretical reconstructions of the historical events that formed those rock layers and fossils, is only about 200 years old. Prior to this, back to ancient Greek times, people had noticed fossils in the rocks. Many believed that the fossils were the remains of former living things turned to stone, and many early Christians (including Tertullian, Chrysostom and Augustine) attributed them to Noah's Flood. But others rejected these ideas and regarded fossils as either jokes of nature, the products of rocks endowed with life in some sense, the creative works of God or perhaps even the deceptions of Satan. The debate was finally settled when Robert Hooke (1635–1703) confirmed by microscopic analysis of fossil wood that fossils were the mineralized remains of former living creatures.

Prior to 1750 one of the most important geological thinkers was Niels Steensen (1638–1686), or Steno, a Dutch anatomist and geologist. He established the principle of superposition, namely that sedimentary rock layers are deposited in a successive, essentially horizontal fashion, so that a lower stratum was deposited before the one above it. In his book *Forerunner* (1669) he expressed belief in a roughly 6,000-year-old Earth and that fossil-bearing rock strata were deposited by Noah's Flood. Over the next century, several authors, including the English geologist John Woodward (1665–1722) and the German geologist Johann Lehmann (1719–1767), wrote books essentially reinforcing that view.

In the latter decades of the 18th century, some French and Italian geologists rejected the biblical account of the Flood and attributed the rock record to natural processes occurring over a long period of time. Several prominent Frenchmen also contributed to the idea of millions of years. The widely respected scientist Comte de Buffon (1707–1788) imagined in his book *Epochs of Nature* (1779) that the earth was once like a hot molten ball that had cooled to reach its present state over about 75,000 years (though his unpublished manuscript says about 3,000,000 years). The astronomer Pierre Laplace (1749–1827) proposed the nebular hypothesis in his *Exposition of the System of the Universe* (1796). This theory said that the solar system was once a hot, spinning gas cloud, which over long ages gradually cooled and condensed to form the planets. Jean Lamarck, a specialist in shell creatures, advocated a theory of biological evolution over long ages in his *Philosophy of Zoology* (1809).

Abraham Werner (1749–1817) was a popular mineralogy professor in Germany. He believed that most of the crust of the earth had been precipitated chemically or mechanically by a slowly receding global ocean over the course of about a million years. It was an elegantly simple theory, but Werner failed to take into account the fossils in the rocks. This was a serious mistake since the fossils tell much about when and how quickly the sediments were deposited and transformed into stone. Many of the greatest geologists of the 19th century were Werner's students, who were impacted by his idea of a very long history for the earth.

In Scotland, James Hutton (1726–1797) was developing a

different theory of Earth history. He studied medicine at the university. After his studies he took over the family farm for a while. But he soon discovered his real love: the study of the earth. In 1788 he published a journal article and in 1795 a book, both by the title *Theory of the Earth*. He proposed that the continents were being slowly eroded into the oceans. Those sediments were gradually hardened by the internal heat of the earth and then raised by convulsions to become new landmasses, which would later be eroded into the oceans, hardened and elevated. So in his view, Earth history was cyclical; and he stated that he could find no evidence of a beginning in the rock record, making Earth history indefinitely long.

CATASTROPHIST—UNIFORMITARIAN DEBATE

Neither Werner nor Hutton paid much attention to the fossils. However, in the early 1800s Georges Cuvier (1768–1832), the famous French comparative anatomist and vertebrate palaeontologist, developed his *catastrophist* theory of Earth history. It was expressed most clearly in his *Discourse on the Revolutions of the Surface of the Globe* (1812). Cuvier believed that over the course of long, untold ages of Earth history, many catastrophic floods of regional or nearly global extent had destroyed and buried creatures in sediments. All but one of these catastrophes occurred before the creation of man.

TFE Graphics

Georges Cuvier
(1768–1832)

William Smith (1769–1839) was a drainage engineer and surveyor, who in the course of his work around Great Britain became fascinated with the strata and fossils. Like Cuvier, he had an old-earth catastrophist view of Earth history. In three works published from 1815 to 1817, he presented the first geological map of England and Wales and explained an order and relative chronology of the rock formations as defined by certain characteristic (index) fossils. He became known as the "Father of English Stratigraphy" because he developed the method of giving relative dates to the rock layers on the basis of the fossils found in them.

A massive blow to catastrophism came during the years 1830 to 1833, when Charles Lyell (1797–1875), a lawyer and former student of Buckland, published his influential three-volume work *Principles of Geology*. Reviving and augmenting the ideas of Hutton, Lyell's *Principles* set forth the principles by which he thought geological interpretations should be made. His theory was a radical *uniformitarianism* in which he insisted that only present-day processes of geological change at *present-day rates of intensity and magnitude* should be used to interpret the rock record of past geological activity. In other words, geological processes of change have been uniform throughout Earth history. No continental or global catastrophic floods have ever occurred, insisted Lyell.

TFE Graphics

Charles Lyell
(1797–1875)

Lyell is often given too much credit (or blame) for destroying faith in the Genesis Flood and the biblical timescale. But we must realize that many Christians (geologists and theologians) contributed to this undermining of biblical teaching before Lyell's book appeared. Although the catastrophist theory had greatly reduced the geological significance of Noah's Flood and expanded Earth history well beyond the traditional biblical view, Lyell's work was the final blow for belief in the Flood. By explaining the whole rock record by slow gradual processes, he thereby reduced the Flood to a geological nonevent. Catastrophism did not die out immediately, although by the late 1830s only a few catastrophists remained, and they believed Noah's Flood was geologically insignificant.

By the end of the 19th century, the age of the earth was considered by all geologists to be in the hundreds of millions of years. Radiometric dating methods began to be developed in 1903, and over the course of the 20th century the age of the earth expanded to 4.5 billion years.

CHRISTIAN RESPONSES TO OLD-EARTH GEOLOGY

During the first half of the nineteenth century the church responded in various ways to these old-earth theories of the catastrophists and uniformitarians. A number of writers in Great Britain (and a few in America), who became known as "scriptural geologists," raised biblical, geological and philosophical arguments against the old-earth theories. Some of them were scientists, some were clergy. Some were both ordained and scientifically well informed, as was common in those days. Many of them were very geologically competent by the standards of their day, both by reading and by their own careful observations of rocks and fossils. They believed that the biblical account of Creation and

TFE Graphics

Thomas Chalmers
(1780–1847)

Noah's Flood explained the rock record far better than the old-earth theories.[1]

Other Christians in the early 1800s quickly accepted the idea of millions of years and tried to fit all this time into Genesis, even though the uniformitarians and catastrophists were still debating and geology was in its infancy as a science. In 1804 Thomas Chalmers (1780–1847), a young Presbyterian pastor, began to preach that Christians should accept the millions of years; and in an 1814 review of Cuvier's book, he proposed that all the time could fit between Genesis 1:1 and 1:2. By that time Chalmers was becoming a highly influential evangelical leader and, consequently, this "gap theory" became very popular. In 1823 the respected Anglican theologian George Stanley Faber (1773–1854) began to advocate the day-age view, namely that the days of creation were not literal but figurative for long ages.

To accept these geological ages, Christians also had to reinterpret the Flood. In the 1820s John Fleming (1785–1857), a Presbyterian minister, contended that Noah's Flood was so peaceful it left no lasting geological evidence. John Pye Smith (1774–1851), a Congregational theologian, preferred to see it as a localized inundation in the Mesopotamian valley (modern-day Iraq).

---

[1] See Mortenson, T., *The Great Turning Point: The Church's Catastrophic Mistake on Geology—Before Darwin* (Master Books, 2004) for a full discussion of these men and the battle they fought against these developing old-earth theories and Christian compromises.

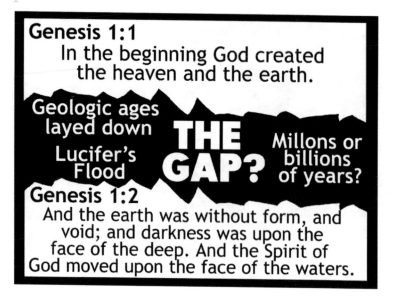

Liberal theology, which by the early 1800s was dominating the church in Europe, was beginning to make inroads into Britain and North America in the 1820s. The liberals considered Genesis 1–11 to be as historically unreliable and unscientific as the creation and flood myths of the ancient Babylonians, Sumerians and Egyptians.

In spite of the efforts of the scriptural geologists, these various old-earth reinterpretations of Genesis prevailed so that by 1845 all the commentaries on Genesis had abandoned the biblical chronology and the global Flood; and by the time of Darwin's *Origin of Species* (1859) the young-earth view had essentially disappeared within the church. From that time onward most Christian leaders and scholars of the church accepted the millions of years and insisted that the age of the earth was not important. Many godly men also soon accepted evolution as well. Space allows only mention of a few examples.

The Baptist "prince of preachers" Charles Spurgeon (1834–

1892) uncritically accepted the old-earth geological theory (though he never explained how to fit the long ages into the Bible). In an 1855 sermon he said,

> Can any man tell me when the beginning was? Years ago we thought the beginning of this world was when Adam came upon it; but we have discovered that thousands of years before that God was preparing chaotic matter to make it a fit abode for man, putting races of creatures upon it, who might die and leave behind the marks of his handiwork and marvelous skill, before he tried his hand on man.[2]

The great Presbyterian theologian at Princeton Seminary Charles Hodge (1779–1878) insisted that the age of the earth was not important. He favored the gap theory initially and switched to the day-age view later in life. His compromise contributed to the eventual victory of liberal theology at Princeton about 50 years after his death.[3]

C. I. Scofield put the gap theory in notes on Genesis 1:2 in his Scofield Reference Bible, which was used by millions of Christians around the world. More recently, a respected Old Testament scholar reasoned,

> From a superficial reading of Genesis 1, the impression would seem to be that the entire creative process took place in six twenty-four-hour days. If this was the true intent of the Hebrew author ... this seems to run counter to modern

---

2   Spurgeon, C.H., Election, *The New Park Street Pulpit* 1:318, 1990.
3   See Pipa, J., and Hall, D., eds., *Did God Create in Six Days?* pp. 7–16, 2005, for some of the documentation of this sad slide into apostasy.

scientific research, which indicates that the
planet Earth was created several billion years
ago ... .[4]

Numerous similar statements from Christian scholars and
leaders in the last few decades could be quoted to show that
their interpretation of Genesis is controlled by the fact that they
assume that geologists have proven millions of years. As a result,
most seminaries and Christian colleges around the world are
compromised.

[4] Archer, G., *A Survey of Old Testament Introduction*, p. 187, 1985.

COMPROMISE UNNECESSARY

The sad irony of all this compromise is that in the last half century, the truth of Genesis 1–11 has been increasingly vindicated, often unintentionally by the work of evolutionists. Lyell's uniformitarian *Principles* dominated geology until about the 1970s, when Derek Ager (1923–1993), a prominent British geologist, and others increasingly challenged Lyell's assumptions and argued that much of the rock record shows evidence of rapid catastrophic erosion or sedimentation, drastically reducing the time involved in the formation of many geological deposits. Ager, an atheist to his death (as far as one can tell from his writings), explained the influence of Lyell on geology this way:

> My excuse for this lengthy and amateur digression into history is that I have been trying to show how I think geology got into the hands of the theoreticians [uniformitarians] who were conditioned by the social and political history of their day more than by observations in the field. ... In other words, we have allowed ourselves to be brain-washed into avoiding any interpretation of the past that involves extreme and what might be termed "catastrophic" processes.[5]

These "neocatastrophist" reinterpretations of the rocks have developed contemporaneously with a resurgence of "Flood geology," a view of Earth history very similar to that of the 19th century scriptural geologists and a key ingredient of young-earth creationism, which was essentially launched into the world by the publication of *The Genesis Flood* (1961) by Drs. John Whitcomb and Henry Morris. This movement is now worldwide in scope,

[5] Ager, D., *The Nature of the Stratigraphical Record*, pp. 46–47, 1981.

and the scientific sophistication of the scientific model is rapidly increasing with time.

Many Christians today are arguing that we need to contend against Darwinism with "intelligent design" arguments and leave Genesis out of the public discussion. But this strategy was tried in the early 19th century with many writings on natural theology, culminating in the famous eight volumes of the 1830s that collectively became known as the *Bridgewater Treatises*. These books were "preaching to the choir" and did nothing to retard the slide in the culture toward atheism and deism. In fact, by compromising on the age of the earth and ignoring Scripture in their defense of Christianity, they actually contributed to the weakening of the church. The same is happening today.

The renowned atheist evolutionist and Harvard University biologist Ernst Mayr said this:

> The [Darwinian] revolution began when it became obvious that the earth was very ancient rather than having been created only 6000 years ago. This finding was the snowball that started the whole avalanche.[6]

Mayr was right about the age of the earth (not Darwin's theory) being the beginning of the avalanche of unbelief. He was wrong that the idea of millions of years was a "finding" of scientific research. Rather, it was the fruit of antibiblical philosophical assumptions used to interpret the rocks and fossils. Historical research has shown that Laplace was an open atheist, that Buffon, Lamarck, Werner and Hutton were deists or atheists, and that Cuvier, William Smith and Lyell were deists or vague theists. These men (who influenced the thinking of compromised

[6] Mayr, E., The nature of the Darwinian revolution, *Science* **176**:988, 1972.

Christians) were NOT unbiased objective pursuers of truth.

Typical of what Lyell, Buffon and others wrote is Hutton's statement. He insisted, "The past history of our globe must be explained by what can be seen to be happening now. ... No powers are to be employed that are not natural to the globe, no action to be admitted except those of which we know the principle."[7] By insisting that geologists must reason only from known, present-day natural processes, Hutton ruled out supernatural creation and the unique global Flood of Genesis, before he ever looked at the rocks.

It is no wonder that Hutton could not see the overwhelming geological evidence confirming the biblical teaching about creation, the Flood and the age of the earth. And no wonder all the geology students who have been brainwashed with the same presuppositions for the last 200 years haven't been able to see it either. We should not be surprised that most Christian leaders and scholars are ignorant of the evidence. They, too, have been brainwashed, as many young-earth creationists once were also.

DISASTROUS CONSEQUENCES OF COMPROMISE

The scriptural geologists of the early 19th century opposed old-earth geological theories not only because the theories reflected erroneous scientific reasoning and were contrary to Scripture, but also because they believed that Christian compromise with such theories would eventually have a catastrophic effect on the health of the church and her witness to a lost world. Henry Cole, an Anglican minister, wrote:

> Many reverend geologists, however, would
> evince their reverence for the divine Revelation

7 Hutton, J., Theory of the Earth, Trans. of the Royal Society of Edinburgh, 1788, quoted in Holmes, A., *Principles of Physical Geology*, pp. 43–44, 1965.

by making a distinction between its *historical* and its *moral* portions; and maintaining, that the latter only is inspired and absolute Truth; but that the former is not so; and therefore is open to any latitude of philosophic and scientific interpretation, modification or denial! According to these impious and infidel modifiers and separators, there is not one third of the Word of God that *is* inspired; for not more, nor perhaps so much, of that Word, is occupied in abstract moral revelation, instruction, and precept. The other two thirds, therefore, are open to any scientific modification and interpretation; or, (if scientifically required,) to a total denial! It may however be safely asserted, that whoever professedly, before men, disbelieves the inspiration of any part of Revelation, disbelieves, in the sight of God, its inspiration altogether. ... What the consequences of such things must be to a revelation-possessing land, time will rapidly and awfully unfold in its opening pages of national skepticism, infidelity, and apostasy, and of God's righteous vengeance on the same![8]

Cole and other opponents of the old-earth theories rightly understood that the historical portions of the Bible (including Genesis 1–11) are foundational to the theological and moral teachings of Scripture. Destroy the credibility of the former and sooner or later you will see rejection of the latter both inside and

---

[8]   Cole, H., *Popular Geology Subversive of Divine Revelation*, pp. ix–x, 44–45 footnote, 1834.

outside the church. If the scriptural geologists were alive today and saw the castle diagram shown below, they would say, "That pictures exactly what we were concerned about!" The history of the once-Christian nations in Europe and North America has confirmed the scriptural geologists' worst fears about the church and society.

It is time for the church, especially her leaders and scholars, to stop ignoring the age of the earth and the scientific evidence that increasingly vindicates the Word of God. The church must repent of her compromise with millions of years and once again believe and preach the literal truth of Genesis 1–11. It is time to take the church back to Genesis.

WHAT'S WRONG
WITH PROGRESSIVE
CREATION?

KEN HAM & DR. TERRY MORTENSON

As we saw in the last chapter, because of the impact of evolutionary thought on our culture, many Christians have compromised with so-called "science" and tried to add millions of years to the Bible. As a result, we have the gap theory, the day-age view, theistic evolution and the framework hypothesis. While these views differ in significant areas, one thing they all have in common is adoption of an evolutionary timescale. Perhaps the most significant movement of late is the view called *progressive creationism*, championed by Dr. Hugh Ross. This chapter will compare Dr. Ross's teachings with the Bible and science and show us the dangers of trying to fit the Bible into modern-day scientific theories.

ONE RESULT OF COMPROMISING WITH our evolutionary culture is the view of creation called the "day-age" theory or "progressive creation." This view, while not a new one, has received wide publicity in the past several years. Much of this publicity is due to the publications and lectures of astronomer Dr. Hugh Ross—probably the world's leading progressive creationist. Dr. Ross's views on how to interpret the book of Genesis won early endorsements from many well-known Christian leaders, churches, seminaries and Christian colleges. The teachings of Dr. Ross seemingly allowed Christians to use the term "creationist" but still gave them supposed academic respectability in the eyes of the world by rejecting six literal days of creation and maintaining billions of years. However, after his views became more fully understood, many who had previously embraced progressive creation realized how bankrupt those views are and removed their endorsement.

In this chapter some of the teachings of progressive creation will be examined in light of Scripture and good science. For a more complete analysis, see the book *Refuting Compromise* by Dr. Jonathan Sarfati.

IN SUMMARY, PROGRESSIVE CREATION TEACHES:

- The big bang origin of the universe occurred about 16 billion years ago.

- The days of creation were overlapping periods of millions and billions of years.

- Over millions of years, God created new species as others kept going extinct.

- The record of nature is just as perfect as the Word of God.

- Death, bloodshed and disease existed before Adam and Eve.

- Manlike creatures that behaved much like us (and painted on cave walls) existed before Adam and Eve but did not have a spirit and thus had no hope of salvation.

- The Genesis Flood was a local event.

THE BIG BANG ORIGIN OF THE UNIVERSE

Progressive creation teaches that the modern big bang theory of the origin of the universe is true and has been proven by scientific inquiry and observation. For Hugh Ross and others like him, big bang cosmology becomes the basis by which the Bible is interpreted. This includes belief that the universe and the earth are billions of years old. Dr. Ross even goes so far as to state that life would not be possible on Earth without billions of years of Earth history:

> It only works in a cosmos of a hundred-billion trillion stars that's precisely sixteen-billion-years old. This is the narrow window of time in which life is possible.[1]

> Life is only possible when the universe is between 12 and 17 billion years.[2]

This, of course, ignores the fact that God is omnipotent—He could make a fully functional universe ready for life right from the beginning, for with God nothing is impossible (Matthew 19:26).[3]

---

[1] Dallas Theological Seminary chapel service, September 13, 1996.
[2] Toccoa Falls Christian College, Staley Lecture Series, March 1997.
[3] For an evaluation of the big bang model, see chapter 6: "Does the big bang fit with the Bible?"

THE DAYS OF CREATION IN GENESIS 1

Progressive creationists claim that the days of creation in Genesis 1 represent long periods of time. In fact, Dr. Ross believes Day 3 of Creation Week lasted more than 3 billion years![4] This assertion is made in order to allow for the billions of years that evolutionists claim are represented in the rock layers of Earth. This position, however, has problems, both biblically and scientifically.

The text of Genesis 1 clearly states that God supernaturally created all that is in six actual days. If we are prepared to let the words of the text speak to us in accord with the context and their normal definitions, without influence from outside ideas, then the word for "day" in Genesis 1 obviously means an ordinary day of about 24 hours. It is qualified by a number, the phrase "evening and morning," and for Day 1, the words "light and darkness."[5]

Dr. James Barr, Regius Professor of Hebrew at Oxford University, who himself does not believe Genesis is true history, admitted that, as far as the language of Genesis 1 is concerned,

> ... so far as I know, there is no professor of Hebrew or Old Testament at any world-class university who does not believe that the writer(s) of Gen. 1–11 intended to convey to their readers the ideas that (a) creation took place in a series of six days which were the same as the days of 24 hours we now experience, (b) the figures contained in the Genesis genealogies provided by simple addition a chronology from the beginning of the world up to later stages in the biblical story, (c)

[4] www.reasons.org/resources/apologetics/creation_timeline_chart/, September 13, 2005.

[5] See *The Answers Book*, chapter 2: "Did God really take six days?" for a more detailed defense of literal days in Genesis 1.

Noah's Flood was understood to be world-wide and extinguish all human and animal life except for those in the ark.[6]

Besides the textual problems, progressive creationists have scientific dilemmas as well. They accept modern scientific measurements for the age of the earth, even though these measurements are based on evolutionary, atheistic assumptions. Dr. Ross often speaks of the "facts of nature" and the "facts of science" when referring to the big bang and billions of years. This demonstrates his fundamental misunderstanding of evidence. The scientific "facts" that evolutionists claim as proof of millions of years are really *interpretations* of selected observations that have been made with *antibiblical, philosophical assumptions.* We all have the same facts: the same living creatures, the same DNA molecules, the same fossils, the same rock layers, the same Grand Canyon, the same moon, the same planets, the same starlight from distant stars and galaxies, etc. These are the facts; how old they are and what they mean are the *interpretations* of the facts. And what one believes about history will affect how one interprets these facts. History is littered with so-called "scientific facts" that supposedly had proven the Bible wrong, but which were shown years or decades later to be not facts but erroneously interpreted observations because of the antibiblical assumptions used.[7]

THE ORDER OF CREATION

As their name indicates, progressive creationists believe that God progressively created species on Earth over billions of years, with new species replacing extinct ones, starting with

---

6 Letter to David C. C. Watson, April 23, 1984.
7 See chapter 12: "What's the best 'proof' of creation?" for more on how our presuppositions influence our interpretations.

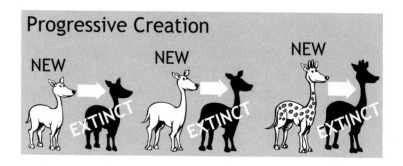

simple organisms and culminating in the creation of Adam and Eve. They accept the evolutionary order for the development of life on Earth, even though this contradicts the order given in the Genesis account of creation. Evolutionary theory holds that the first life forms were marine organisms, while the Bible says that God created land plants first. Reptiles are supposed to have pre-dated birds, while Genesis says that birds came first. Evolutionists believe that land mammals came before whales, while the Bible teaches that God created whales first.

Dr. Davis Young, former geology professor at Calvin College, recognized this dilemma and abandoned the "day-age" theory. Here is part of his explanation as to why he discarded it:

> The biblical text, for example, has vegetation appearing on the third day and animals on the fifth day. Geology, however, had long realized that invertebrate animals were swarming in the seas long before vegetation gained a foothold on the land … . Worse yet, the text states that on the fourth day God made the heavenly bodies after the earth was already in existence. Here is

a blatant confrontation with science. Astronomy insists that the sun is older than the earth.[8]

THE SIXTY-SEVENTH BOOK OF THE BIBLE

Dr. Ross has stated that he believes nature to be "just as perfect" as the Bible. Here is the full quote:

> Not everyone has been exposed to the sixty-six books of the Bible, but everyone on planet Earth has been exposed to the sixty-seventh book—the book that God has written upon the heavens for everyone to read.

> And the Bible tells us it's impossible for God to lie, so the record of nature must be just as perfect, and reliable and truthful as the sixty-six books of the Bible that is part of the Word of God ... . And so when astronomers tell us [their attempts to measure distance in space] ... it's part of the truth that God has revealed to us. It actually encompasses part of the Word of God.[9]

CREATIONWISE

WHICH ONE ARE YOU GOING TO TRUST?

HOLY BIBLE

OR

Evolution BELIEF
1998 Edition

It is REWRITTEN and REWRITTEN and REWRITTEN and *Rewritten* and...

"IT IS WRITTEN" MATT. 4:4

---

8 Young, D., *The Harmonization of Scripture and Science*, science symposium at Wheaton College, March 23, 1990.

9 Ref. 2.

Dr. Ross is right that God cannot lie, and God tells us in Romans 8:22 that "the whole creation groans and labors with birth pangs" because of sin. And not only was the universe cursed, but man himself has been affected by the Fall. So how can sinful, fallible human beings in a sin-cursed universe say that their interpretation of the evidence is as perfect as God's written revelation? Scientific assertions must use *fallible* assumptions and *fallen* reasoning—how can this be the Word of God?

The respected systematic theologian Louis Berkhof said,

> Since the entrance of sin into the world, man can gather true knowledge about God from His general revelation only if he studies it in the light of Scripture, in which the elements of God's original self-revelation, which were obscured and perverted by the blight of sin, are republished, corrected, and interpreted. ... Some are inclined to speak of God's general revelation as a second source; but this is hardly correct in view of the fact that nature can come into consideration here only as interpreted in the light of Scripture.[10]

In other words, Christians should build their thinking on the Bible, not on "science."

DEATH AND DISEASE BEFORE ADAM

Progressive creationists believe the fossil record was formed from the millions of animals that lived and died before Adam and Eve were created. They accept the idea that there was death, bloodshed and disease (including cancer) before sin, which goes directly against the teaching of the Bible and dishonors the character of God.

---

[10] Berkhof, L., Introductory volume to *Systematic Theology*, pp. 60, 96, 1946.

God created a perfect world at the beginning. When He was finished, God stated that His creation was "very good." The Bible makes it clear that man and all the animals were vegetarians before the Fall (Genesis 1:29). Plants were given to them for food (plants do not have a *nephesh* [life spirit] as man and animals do and thus eating them would not constitute "death" in the biblical sense[11]).

Concerning the entrance of sin into the world, Dr. Ross writes, "The groaning of creation in anticipation of release from sin has lasted fifteen billion years and affected a hundred billion trillion stars."[12]

---

[11] See *The Answers Book*, chapter 6: "How did bad things come about?" for more details.

[12] *Facts for Faith*, Issue 8, 2002.

However, the Bible teaches something quite different. The Apostle Paul states, "Through one man sin entered the world, and death through sin" (Romans 5:12). It is clear that there was no sin in the world before Adam sinned, and thus no death.

God killed the first animal in the Garden and shed blood because of sin—if there was death, bloodshed, disease and suffering before sin, then the basis for the Atonement is *destroyed*. Christ suffered death because death was the penalty for sin. There will be no death or suffering in the perfect "restoration"—so why can't we accept the same in a perfect ("very good") creation before sin?

God must be quite incompetent and cruel to make things in the way that evolutionists imagine the universe and earth to have evolved, as most creatures that ever existed died cruel deaths. Progressive creation denigrates the wisdom and goodness of God by suggesting that this was God's method of creation. This view attacks His truthfulness as well. If God really created over the course of billions of years, then He has misled most believers for 4,000 years into believing that He did it in six days.

SPIRITLESS HOMINIDS BEFORE ADAM

Since evolutionary radiometric dating methods have dated certain humanlike fossils as older than Ross's date for modern humans (approx. 40,000 years), he and other progressive creationists insist that these are fossils of pre-Adamic creatures that had no spirit, and thus no salvation.

Dr. Ross accepts and defends these evolutionary dating methods, so he must redefine all evidence of humans (descendants of Noah) if they are given evolutionary dates of more than about 40,000 years (e.g., the Neandertal cave sites) as related to spiritless "hominids," which the Bible does not mention. However, these same methods have been used to "date" the Australian Aborigines

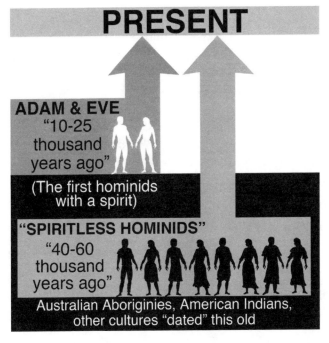

back at least 60,000 years (some have claimed much older) and fossils of "anatomically modern humans" to over 100,000 years.[13] By Ross's reasoning, none of these (including the Australian Aborigines) could be descendants of Adam and Eve. However, Acts 17:26 says, "And He has made from one blood every nation of men to dwell on all the face of the earth, and has determined their preappointed times and the boundaries of their dwellings." All people on Earth are descendants of Adam.

In addition, the fossil record cannot, by its very nature, conclusively reveal if a creature had a spirit or not, since spirits are not fossilized. But there is clear evidence that creatures, which Ross (following the evolutionists) places before Adam, had art and clever technology and that they buried their dead in a way

---

13 White, T., *et. al.*, Pleistocene *Homo sapiens* from Middle Awash, Ethiopia, *Nature* **423**:742-747, June 12, 2003.

that many of Adam's descendants have. Therefore, we have strong reason to believe that they were fully human and actually descendants of Adam, and that they lived only a few thousand years ago.

THE GENESIS FLOOD

One important tenet of progressive creation is that the Flood of Noah's day was a local flood, limited to the Mesopotamian region. They believe that the rock layers and fossils found around the world are the result of billions of years of evolutionary Earth history, rather than from the biblical Flood.

Dr. Ross often says that he believes in a "universal" or "worldwide" flood, but in reality he does not believe that the Flood covered the whole earth. He argues that the text of Genesis 7 doesn't really say that the Flood covered the whole earth. But read it for yourself:

> 19 They [the flood waters] rose greatly on the earth, and *all* the high mountains under the *entire* heavens were covered. ...
> 21 *Every* living thing that moved on the earth perished—birds, livestock, wild animals, *all* the creatures that swarm over the earth, and *all* mankind.
> 22 *Everything* on dry land that had the breath of life in its nostrils died.

23 *Every* living thing on the face of the earth was wiped out; men and animals and the creatures that move along the ground and the birds of the air were wiped from the earth. *Only* Noah was left, and those with him in the ark [emphasis added].

Also, many questions remain for those who teach that the Genesis Flood was only local:

- If the Flood were local, why did Noah have to build an Ark? He could have walked to the other side of the mountains and missed it.

- If the Flood were local, why did God send the animals to the Ark so they could escape death? There would have been other animals to reproduce that kind if these particular ones had died.

- If the Flood were local, why was the Ark big enough to hold all the different kinds of vertebrate land animals? If only Mesopotamian animals were aboard, the Ark could have been much smaller.[14]

- If the Flood were local, why would birds have been sent on board? These could simply have winged across to a nearby mountain range.

- If the Flood were local, how could the waters rise to 15 cubits (8 meters) above the mountains (Genesis 7:20)? Water seeks its own level. It couldn't rise to cover the local mountains while

---

[14] See *The Answers Book*, chapter 13: "How did the animals fit on Noah's Ark?"

leaving the rest of the world untouched.

- If the Flood were local, people who did not happen to be living in the vicinity would not be affected by it. They would have escaped God's judgment on sin. If this had happened, what did Christ mean when He likened the coming judgment of all men to the judgment of "all" men in the days of Noah (Matthew 24:37–39)? A partial judgment in Noah's day means a partial judgment to come.

- If the Flood were local, God would have repeatedly broken His promise never to send such a flood again.

CONCLUSION

It is true that whether one believes in six literal days does not ultimately affect one's salvation, if one is truly born again. However, we need to stand back and look at the "big picture." In many nations the Word of God was once widely respected and taken seriously. But once the door of compromise is unlocked and Christian leaders concede that we shouldn't take the Bible as written in Genesis, why should the world take heed of it in *any* area? Because the church has told the world that one can use man's interpretation of the world (such as billions of years) to reinterpret the Bible, it is seen as an outdated, scientifically incorrect "holy book," not intended to be taken seriously.

As each subsequent generation has pushed this door of compromise open further and further, increasingly they are not accepting the morality or salvation of the Bible either. After all, if the history in Genesis is not correct as written, how can one be sure the rest can be taken as written? Jesus said, "If I have told you earthly things, and you do not believe, how will you believe if I tell you of heavenly things?" (John 3:12).

It would not be exaggerating to claim that the majority of Christian leaders and laypeople within the church today do not believe in six literal days. Sadly, being influenced by the world has led to the church no longer powerfully influencing the world.

The "war of the worldviews" is not ultimately one of young earth versus old earth, or billions of years versus six days, or creation versus evolution—the real battle is the authority of the Word of God versus man's fallible theories.

Belief in a historical Genesis is important because progressive creation and its belief in millions of years (1) contradicts the clear teaching of Scripture, (2) assaults the character of God, (3) severely damages and distorts the Bible's teaching on death and (4) undermines the gospel by undermining the clear teaching of Genesis, which gives the whole basis for Christ's Atonement and our need for a Redeemer. So ultimately, the issue of a literal Genesis is about the authority of the Word of God versus the authority of the words of sinful men.

Why do Christians believe in the bodily Resurrection of Jesus Christ? Because of the *words of Scripture* ("according to the Scriptures").

And why should Christians believe in six literal days of creation? Because of the *words of Scripture* ("In six days the Lord made …").

The real issue is one of authority—let us unashamedly stand upon God's Word as our sole authority!

Is the intelligent design movement Christian?

DR. GEORGIA PURDOM

"This textbook contains material on evolution. Evolution is a theory, not a fact, regarding the origin of living things. This material should be approached with an open mind, studied carefully and critically considered." Such was the text of a "warning sticker" that was approved by the Cobb County Board of Education (Georgia) for some high-school biology textbooks. After a legal battle, a federal judge ruled the stickers were unconstitutional because they endorse a religion. The battle to allow alternatives to Darwinian evolution in our schools is in high gear. One proposed alternative is Intelligent Design (ID). In this chapter, we take a look at the positives and negatives of the ID movement, and in the end see that all theories that leave out the Bible are deficient.

ONE PLAYER IN THE "WAR of the worldviews" is the intelligent design movement. ID has gained increasing recognition and publicity over the last several years at both local and national levels. It is especially well known in educational circles, where it has been heralded as an alternative to Darwinism/naturalism.

Intelligent design can be defined as a theory which holds that "certain features" of living things were designed by an "intelligent cause" as opposed to being formed through purely natural means.[1] The ID theory does not name the intelligent cause, and it does not claim that everything is designed, thus allowing for evolution/natural causes to play a role.

The historical roots of the ID movement lie in the natural theology movement of the 18th and 19th centuries. William Paley (1743–1805) reasoned that if one walked across a field and came upon a watch, the assumption would be that there had to be a watchmaker—the complexity and purpose of the watch points to the fact that it is not the result of undirected, unintelligent causes, but the product of a designer.[2] Natural theology sought to support the existence of God through nature (general revelation) apart from the Bible (special revelation), since the Bible was facing much criticism at that time. The scientific knowledge of that time was grossly deficient, and it was thought that natural causes were sufficient to bring everything into existence.

In the last 100 years or so there has been an explosion of knowledge about the complexity of cells, DNA and microorganisms. Thus, the need for a designer has become even greater. The current ID movement has more than just philosophical

---

[1] Discovery Institute Center for Science and Culture, www.discovery.org/csc/topQuestions.php, September 13, 2005.

[2] Cooper, B., (Ed.), *Paley's Watchmaker: An abridged edition of Wm Paley's "Natural Theology"* (first published in 1802), pp. 29–31, 1997.

arguments for a designer; it uses scientific evidence drawn from biology, chemistry and physics.

IRREDUCIBLE COMPLEXITY

The ID concept affirms that living things are designed and exhibit *irreducible complexity*. Some examples are the biochemistry of vision and the mammalian blood-clotting pathway. These biological pathways consist of many factors, and *all* the factors are necessary for the pathway to function properly. Thus evolution (which works via the mechanism of small, gradual steps that keep only that which is immediately functional) could not have formed these pathways. For example, if only three of the blood-clotting factors (there are many factors in the complete pathway) were formed in an organism, blood would not clot, and thus the factors would not be kept because they are not currently useful to the organism. Evolutionary processes do not allow the organism to keep the three factors in the hopes that one day the rest of the blood-clotting factors will form. Evolution is goalless and purposeless; therefore, it does not keep the leftovers.

The question of whether or not a feature of a living organism displays design can be answered by using what is called an "explanatory filter." The filter has three levels of explanation:

1. Necessity—did it have to happen?

2. Chance—did it happen by accident?

3. Design—did an intelligent agent cause it to happen?

This is a very logical, common-sense approach used by individuals everyday to deduce cause and effect. For example, consider the scenario of a woman falling.

1.   Did she have to fall? No, but she did.

2.   Was it an accident?

3.   Or was she pushed?

If we apply this explanatory filter to living organisms, a feature must be designed if the first two answers are no.

Let us evaluate the blood-clotting pathway with respect to these three questions:

1.   The blood-clotting pathway is compatible with, but not required by, the natural laws of biology and chemistry; so it is not a necessity specified by natural phenomena.

2.   It is complex because it is composed of many factors, thus the remote probability that it happened by chance. (Note that complex structures fall into two categories: ordered complexity and specified complexity. A snowflake, although complex structurally, has little information and thus is considered an example of ordered complexity. It is the direct result of natural phenomena rather than intelligent design[3]).

3.   The blood-clotting pathway does show design, referred to as specified complexity, because it is complex and has a high amount of information. It is the direct result of an intelligent agent. All the factors must be present and interact with each other in a specified manner in order for the

[3]   See www.intelligentdesign.org/menu/complex/complex3.htm for a more detailed discussion.

pathway to be functional. Thus, the blood-clotting pathway meets all the requirements for irreducible complexity, and so must be designed.

WHAT THE ID MOVEMENT IS AND IS NOT

William Dembski states, "ID is three things: a scientific research program that investigates the effects of intelligent causes; an intellectual movement that challenges Darwinism and its naturalistic legacy; and a way of understanding divine action."[4] The ID theory focuses on what is designed rather than answering the questions of who, when, why and how. Those within the movement believe this promotes scientific endeavor by looking for function and purpose in those things that are designed, whereas an evolutionary mindset presupposes waste and purposelessness and aborts further scientific thinking. Although it may be a way of understanding divine action outside of a biblical framework, there are some serious implications for the Creator, which we will discuss later.

The ID movement does not speak to the optimality of design because it does not attempt to explain all designs. Remember, only "certain features" are designed, and evolutionary processes are not ruled out. The ID movement also claims not to be religiously motivated. It focuses not on the whom but on the what. This may sound very appealing at first glance. Some biblical creationists believe that the ID movement's tolerance and acceptance of a wide range of beliefs about the supernatural could be useful in reaching a larger audience. Since the movement is very careful not to associate itself with Christianity or any formal religion, some think it will stand a better chance of gaining acceptance as an alternative to Darwinism in the schools, because it does not violate the so-

---

4   Dembski, W., Science and design, *First Things* **86**:21–27.

called "separation of church and state."

The ID movement does have several positives. The movement has produced many resources, including books and multimedia, which support the biblical creationist viewpoint. It makes clear that Darwinism/naturalism is based on the presupposition that the supernatural does not exist, thus affecting the way one interprets the scientific evidence. ID is based on the presupposition that the supernatural does exist.

ID may serve as a useful tool in *preliminary* discussions about God and creation to gain an audience that might be turned off at the mention of the Bible. However, in further discussions, the Bible as the biblical creationists' foundation should be primary.[5]

---

[5]   See *AiG's views on the Intelligent Design Movement*, www. AnswersInGenesis.org/ID.

However, the central problem with the ID movement is a divorce of the Creator from creation. The Creator and His creation cannot be separated; they reflect on each other. All other problems within the movement stem from this one.

Those within the ID movement claim their science is neutral. However, science is not neutral because it works with hypotheses based on beliefs or presuppositions. It is ironic that they refuse to see this about their own science, considering that they claim the problem with Darwinism is the presupposition that nothing supernatural exists. All scientists approach their work with presuppositions. The question is whether those beliefs are rooted in man's fallible ideas about the past or rooted in the infallible Word of God, the Bible.

The natural theology movement of the 1800s failed because it did not answer the next logical question: If it is designed, then who designed it? Although most within this movement claimed that design pointed to the God of the Bible, by divorcing general revelation (nature) from special revelation (the Bible), they opened the door to other conclusions. Deism (another movement of the same period) took the idea of excluding the Bible to the extreme and said God can only be known through nature and human reason, and that faith and revelation do not exist.

In today's culture, many are attracted to the ID movement because they can decide for themselves who the creator is—a Great Spirit, Brahman, Allah, God, etc. The current movement does not have unity on the naming of the creator and focuses more on what is designed. Thus, they do not oppose an old age for the earth and allow evolution to play a vital role once the designer formed the basics of life. They fail to understand that a belief in long ages for the earth formed the foundation of Darwinism. If God's Word is not true concerning the age of the earth, then

maybe it's not true concerning other events of the Creation Week, and maybe God was not a necessary part of the equation for life after all.

The ID movement's belief in evolution also allows them to distance themselves from the problem of evil in the natural world. Examples of this include pathogenic microbes, carnivorous animals, disease and death.

Without the framework of the Bible and the understanding that evil entered the world through man's actions (Genesis 3), God appears sloppy and incompetent, if not downright vicious. People ask why God is unable to prevent evil from thwarting His plans, resulting in such poor design, instead of understanding that because of the Fall there is now a "cursed" design. In addition, because the ID movement does not acknowledge God as Redeemer, there seems to be no final solution for the evil in this world, and by all appearances evil will continue to reign supreme. However, when we trust the Bible, we read that Jesus clearly conquered death by His Resurrection (Romans 6:3–10) and one day death will no longer reign (Revelation 21:4). Again, the Creator and His creation cannot be separated.

The attributes of God are very important when resolving apparent discrepancies in His creation. For example, according to the Bible the earth is around 6,000 years old. However, starlight can be seen from stars millions of light years away. Also according to the Bible, God does not lie. Therefore, we must lack some information that would resolve this apparent discrepancy. (Some good research has been done on this issue, and there are several plausible solutions.[6])

OUR CREATOR AND REDEEMER

Romans 1:20 states that all men know about God through His creation. However, just recognizing that there is a designer is only the first step. Colossians 1:15–20 and 1 Peter 3:3–6 point to the inexorable link between God's role as Creator *and* Redeemer. In Colossians, Paul talks about God as Creator and moves seamlessly to His role as Redeemer. Paul sees creation as a foundation for redemption. In 1 Peter, Peter states that people started disbelieving in the Second Coming of Christ because they started doubting God's role as Creator. Again, God's role as Creator becomes foundational to His role as Redeemer. Recognizing a designer is not enough to be saved; submitting to the Redeemer is also necessary. While some might consider ID to be a noble attempt to counter the evolutionary indoctrination of our culture, it falls far short of a thoroughly biblical response.

---

[6] See Humphreys, D., *Starlight and Time*, 1994; and *The Answers Book*, chapter 5: "How can we see distant stars in a young universe?"

AFTER EDEN
by Dan Lietha

For since the creation of the world God's invisible attributes, His eternal power and divine nature, have been clearly seen, being understood through what has been made, so that they are without excuse. Romans 1:20

We must not separate the creation from its Creator; knowledge of God must come through both general revelation (nature) and special revelation (the Bible). The theologian Louis Berkhof said, "… since the entrance of sin into the world, man can gather true knowledge about God from His general revelation only if he studies it in the light of Scripture."[7] It is only then that the *entire* truth about God and what is seen around us can be fully understood and used to help people understand the bad news in Genesis and the good news of Jesus Christ.

7 Berkhof, L., Introductory volume to *Systematic Theology*, pp. 60, 1946.

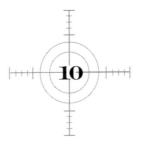

CAN CREATIONISTS BE "REAL" SCIENTISTS?

DR. JASON LISLE

In any serious street fight there is name-calling. And the war of the worldviews is no different. Hollywood has often portrayed Christians as ignorant, mean-spirited Bible-thumpers, while skeptics are depicted as reasonable, intelligent thinkers. Some evolutionists have stated that those who believe in creation cannot be real scientists. Any use of science to support the biblical view of creation is called "pseudoscience." But what is the truth? Are there scientists who believe in creation and do real science? You bet there are. In this chapter, we'll meet some of the great men and women of science, past and present, who are real scientists and who believe the Bible's account of origins. And we'll see that true operational science has nothing to do with evolution.

SOME EVOLUTIONISTS HAVE STATED THAT creationists cannot be real scientists. Several years ago, the National Academy of Sciences published a guidebook entitled *Teaching about Evolution and the Nature of Science.*[1] This guidebook states that biological evolution is "the most important concept in modern biology, a concept essential to understanding key aspects of living things." Famous geneticist Theodosius Dobzhansky stated that "nothing in biology makes sense except in the light of evolution."[2]

But is a belief in particles-to-people evolution really necessary to understand biology and other sciences? Is it even helpful? Have any technological advances been made because of a belief in evolution?

Although evolutionists interpret the evidence in light of their belief in evolution, science works perfectly well without any connection to evolution. Think about it this way: is a belief in molecules-to-man evolution necessary to understand how planets orbit the sun, how telescopes operate or how plants and animals function? Has any biological or medical research benefited from a belief in evolution? Not at all. In fact, the Ph.D. cell biologist (and creationist) Dr. David Menton has stated, "The fact is that though widely believed, evolution contributes nothing to our understanding of empirical science and thus plays no essential role in biomedical research or education."[3] And creationists are not the only ones who understand this. Dr. Philip Skell, Emeritus Evan Pugh Professor of Chemistry, Penn State University, wrote:

---

[1] The claims made in this guidebook have been refuted in Dr. Jonathan Sarfati's powerful book *Refuting Evolution*, available from www.AnswersBookstore.com.
[2] *The American Biology Teacher* 35:125–129.
[3] www.AnswersInGenesis.org/docs2003/0612menton_testimony.asp.

I recently asked more than 70 eminent researchers if they would have done their work differently
if they had thought Darwin's theory was wrong.
The responses were all the same: No.

I also examined the outstanding biodiscoveries
of the past century: the discovery of the double
helix; the characterization of the ribosome; the
mapping of genomes; research on medications
and drug reactions; improvements in food production and sanitation; the development of new
surgeries; and others. I even queried biologists
working in areas where one would expect the
Darwinian paradigm to have most benefited
research, such as the emergence of resistance to
antibiotics and pesticides. Here, as elsewhere, I
found that Darwin's theory had provided no dis-
cernible guidance, but was brought in, after the
breakthroughs, as an interesting narrative gloss … .
From my conversations with leading researchers
it had became [*sic*] clear that modern experimental biology gains its strength from the availability
of new instruments and methodologies, not from
an immersion in historical biology.[4]

The rise of technology is not due to a belief in evolution, either.
Computers, cellular phones and DVD players all operate based
on the laws of physics, which God created. It is because God created a logical, orderly universe and gave us the ability to reason
and to be creative that technology is possible. How can a belief
in evolution (that complex biological machines do *not* require an

---

[4]   Skell, P., Why do we invoke Darwin? *The Scientist* **16**:10.

intelligent designer) aid in the development of complex machines which are clearly intelligently designed? Technology has shown us that sophisticated machines require intelligent designers—not random chance. Science and technology are perfectly consistent with the Bible, but not with evolution.

DIFFERING ASSUMPTIONS

The main difference between scientists who are creationists and those who are evolutionists is their starting assumptions. Creationists and evolutionists have a different view of history, but the way they do science in the present is the same. Both creationists and evolutionists use observation and experimentation to draw conclusions about nature. This is the nature of observational science. It involves repeatable experimentation and observations in the present. Since observational scientific theories are capable of being tested in the present, creationists and evolutionists are generally in agreement on these models. They agree on the nature of gravity, the composition of stars, the speed of light in a vacuum, the size of the solar system, the principles of electricity, etc. These things can be checked and tested in the present.

But historical events cannot be checked scientifically in the present. This is because we do not have access to the past; it is gone. All that we have is the circumstantial evidence (relics) of past events. Although we can make educated guesses about the past and can make inferences from things like fossils and rocks, we cannot directly test our conclusions because we cannot repeat the past. Furthermore, since creationists and evolutionists have very different views of history, it is not surprising that they reconstruct past events very differently. We all have the same evidence; but in order to draw conclusions about what the evidence means, we use our worldview—our most basic beliefs about the nature of reality. Since they have different starting assumptions, creationists and evolutionists interpret the same evidence to mean very different things.

Ultimately, biblical creationists accept the recorded history of the Bible as their starting point. Evolutionists reject recorded history, and have effectively made up their own pseudo-history, which they use as a starting point for interpreting evidence. Both are using their beliefs about the past to interpret the evidence in the present. When we look at the scientific evidence today, we find that it is very consistent with biblical history and not as consistent with millions of years of evolution. We've seen in this book that the scientific evidence is consistent with biblical creation. We've seen that the geological evidence is consistent with a global Flood—not millions of years of gradual deposition. We've seen that the changes in DNA are consistent with the loss of information we would expect as a result of the Curse described in Genesis 3, not the hypothetical gain of massive quantities of genetic information required by molecules-to-man evolution. Real science confirms the Bible.

REAL SCIENTISTS

It shouldn't be surprising that there have been many *real* scientists who believed in biblical creation. Consider Isaac Newton (1642–1727), who codiscovered calculus, formulated the laws of motion and gravity, computed the nature of planetary orbits, invented the reflecting telescope and made a number of discoveries in optics. Newton had profound knowledge of, and faith in, the Bible. Carl Linnaeus (1707–1778), the Swedish botanist who developed the double-Latin-name system for taxonomic classification of plants and animals, also believed the Genesis creation account. So also did the Dutch geologist Nicolaus Steno (1631–1686), who

Isaac Newton
(1642–1727)

developed the basic principles of stratigraphy.

Even in the early 19th century when the idea of millions of years was developed, there were prominent Bible-believing English scientists, such as chemists Andrew Ure (1778–1857) and John Murray (1786?–1851), entomologist William Kirby (1759–1850), and geologist George Young (1777–1848). James Clerk Maxwell (1831–1879) discovered the four fundamental equations that light and all forms of electromagnetic radiation obey. Indeed, Maxwell's equations are what make radio transmissions possible. He was a deep student of Scripture and was firmly opposed to evolution. These and many other great scientists have believed the Bible as the infallible Word of God, and it was their Christian faith that was the driving motivation and intellectual foundation of their excellent scientific work.

Today there are many other Ph.D. scientists who reject evolution and believe that God created in six days, a few thousand years ago, just as recorded in Scripture. Russ Humphreys, a Ph.D. physicist, has developed (among many other things) a model to compute the present strength of planetary magnetic fields,[5] which enabled him to accurately predict the field strengths of the outer planets. Did a belief in the Bible hinder his research? Not at all. On the contrary, Dr. Humphreys was able to make these predictions precisely because he started from the principles of Scripture. John

---

[5] www.creationresearch.org/crsq/articles/21/21_3/21_3.html.

Baumgardner, a Ph.D. geophysicist and biblical creationist, has a sophisticated computer model of catastrophic plate tectonics, which was reported in the journal *Nature*; the assumptions for this model are based on the global Flood recorded in Genesis. Additionally, think of all the people who have benefited from a Magnetic Resonance Imaging (MRI) scan. The MRI scanner was developed by the creationist Dr. Raymond Damadian.[6]

Dr. John Baumgardner

Consider the biblical creationist Georgia Purdom (one of the authors of this book) who has a Ph.D. in molecular genetics. Dr. Purdom certainly understands DNA, mutations and natural selection. However, she is convinced that these do not support evolution because such processes go in the "wrong direction" to make evolution work.[7] On the contrary, they confirm biblical creation.

I have a Ph.D. from a secular university and have done extensive research in solar astrophysics. In my Ph.D. research, I made a number of discoveries about the nature of near-surface solar flows, including the detection of a never-before-seen polar alignment of supergranules, as well as patterns indicative of giant overturning cells. Was I hindered in my research by the conviction that the early chapters of Genesis are literally true? No, it's just the reverse. It is because a logical God created and ordered the universe that I, and other creationists, expect to be able to understand aspects of that universe through logic, careful observation and experimentation.

6   www.AnswersInGenesis.org/creation/v16/i3/science.asp.
7   www.AnswersInGenesis.org/creation/v24/i2/evolution_train.asp.

Clearly, creationists can indeed be real scientists. And this shouldn't be surprising since the very basis for scientific research is biblical creation. This is not to say that noncreationists cannot be scientists. But, in a way, an evolutionist is being inconsistent when he or she does science. The big bang supporter claims the universe is a random chance event, and yet he or she studies it as if it were logical and orderly. The evolutionist is thus forced to borrow certain creationist principles in order to do science. The universe is logical and orderly because its Creator is logical and has imposed order on the universe. God created our minds and gave us the ability and curiosity to study the universe. Furthermore, we can trust that the universe will obey the same physics tomorrow as it does today because God is consistent. This is why science is possible. On the other hand, if the universe is just an accidental product of a big bang, why should it be orderly? Why should there be laws of nature if there is no lawgiver? If our brains are the byproducts of random chance, why should we trust that their conclusions are accurate? But if our minds have been designed, and if the universe has been constructed by God, as the Bible teaches, then of course we should be able to study nature. Science is possible because the Bible is true.

HOW SHOULD A CHRISTIAN RESPOND TO "GAY MARRIAGE"?

KEN HAM

What do the TV shows *ER*, *Will & Grace* and *Desperate Housewives* have in common? They all portray homosexual behavior as a normal and acceptable lifestyle. Television sitcoms, network news and our public education system bombard us with the message of tolerance for gays and lesbians. Many states are debating same-sex marriage initiatives, and the US Government is considering the Federal Marriage Amendment, which would define marriage as the union between a man and a woman only. What does the Bible say about gay marriage? How should a Christian respond to this issue? These are the questions we will tackle in this chapter as we learn how to think biblically about moral issues.

MOST PEOPLE HAVE HEARD OF the account of Adam and Eve. According to the first book of the Bible, Genesis, these two people were the first humans from whom all others in the human race descended. Genesis also records the names of three of Adam and Eve's many children—Cain, Abel and Seth.

Christians claim that this account of human history is accurate, because the Bible itself claims that it is the authoritative Word of the Creator God, without error.

To challenge Christians' faith in the Bible as an infallible revelation from God to humans, many skeptics have challenged the Bible's trustworthiness as a historical document by asking questions like, "Where did Cain find his wife?" (Don't worry—this will become highly relevant to the topic of gay marriage shortly!)

This question of Cain's wife is one of the most-asked questions about the Christian faith and the Bible's reliability. In short, Genesis 5:4 states that Adam had "other sons and daughters"; thus, originally, brothers had to marry sisters.[1]

AN ATHEIST ON A TALK SHOW

This background is helpful in offering the context of a conversation I had with a caller on a radio talk show. The conversation went something like this:

---

[1] For a more detailed answer to this question, see www.AnswersInGenesis. org/Cains_wife.

Caller: "I'm an atheist, and I want to tell you Christians that if you believe Cain married his sister, then that's immoral."

AiG: "If you're an atheist, then that means you don't believe in any personal God, right?"

Caller: "Correct!"

AiG: "Then if you don't believe in God, you don't believe there's such a thing as an absolute authority. Therefore, you believe everyone has a right to their own opinions—to make their own rules about life if they can get away with it, correct?"

Caller: "Yes, you're right."

AiG: "Then, sir, you can't call me immoral; after all, you're an atheist, who doesn't believe in any absolute authority."

The AiG guest went on: "Do you believe all humans evolved from apelike ancestors?"

Caller: "Yes, I certainly believe evolution is fact."

AiG: "Then, sir, from your perspective on life, if man is just some sort of animal who evolved, and if there's no absolute authority, then marriage is whatever you want to define it to be—if you can get away with it in the culture you live in.

"It could be two men, two women or one man and ten women; in fact, it doesn't even have to be a man with another human—it could be a man with an animal.[2]

"I'm sorry, sir, that you think Christians have a problem. I think it's you who has the problem. Without an absolute authority, marriage, or any other aspect of how to live in society, is determined on the basis of opinion and ultimately could be anything one decides—if the culture as a whole will allow you to get away with this. You have the problem, not me."

It was a fascinating—and revealing—exchange.

So the question, then, that could be posed to this caller and other skeptics is this: "Who has the right to determine what is good or bad, or what is morally right or wrong in the culture? Who determines whether marriage as an institution should be adhered to, and if so, what the rules should be?"

THE "PRAGMATICS" ASPECT OF OPPOSING GAY MARRIAGE—SOME CAUTIONS

Some who defend marriage as a union between one man and one woman claim that it can be shown that cultures that have not adhered to this doctrine have reaped all sorts of problems (whether the spread of diseases or other issues). Thus, they claim, on this basis, it's obvious that marriage should be between one man and one woman only.

---

2   See Man marries dog for luck—then dies, www.theage.com.au/ articles/2004/02/04/1075853937098.html?from=storyrhs and Bates, M., Marriage in the new millennium: love, honor and scratch between the ears, *Oak Lawn (Illinois) Reporter*, April 5, 2001, as referenced at www. freerepublic.com/forum/a3ac9e00d0a87.htm. There are many articles online that discuss the possibility of a man marrying his dog if the sanctity of marriage is not upheld; search for words like *marriage, man* and *dog*.

Even though such problems as the spread of HIV might be shown to be a sound argument in this issue, ultimately it's not a good basis for stating that one man for one woman must be the rule. It may be a sound argument based on the pragmatics of wanting to maintain a healthy physical body, but why should one or more human beings have the right to dictate to others what they can or can't do in sexual relationships? After all, another person might decide that the relationship between one man and woman in marriage might cause psychological problems and use that as the basis for the argument. So which one is correct?

Say that a person used the argument that research has shown, for example, that the children of gay parents had a higher incidence of depression. Or the argument that since HIV kills people, it is vital that marriage is between a man and a woman. But note how such arguments have also been tried in the case of abortion and *rejected* by the culture.

Let us illustrate. Some researchers claim to have shown a high incidence of depression in people who have had an abortion. The culture, however, has rejected such pragmatic "we shouldn't hurt people" arguments, claiming that it is more important that others have the "right to choose." The argument that abortion kills people is an important one because most people still accept the basic biblical prohibition against taking innocent human life. So we should ensure that people know that the baby is really

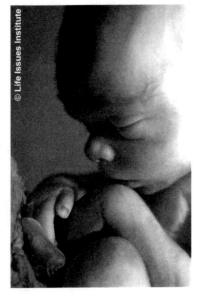

© Life Issues Institute

human. But is it going to be enough in the long term, as even this prohibition cannot be absolute without the Bible?

THE MORALS OF THE MAJORITY

Over the centuries in our Western nations, people (including their leaders) almost universally accepted the belief that marriage was to be one man for one woman. In recent times, that once-prevailing view has been shifting—and rapidly.

What has brought about this change in the past few decades? The answer can be boiled down to how one considers this question: Who in society determines what is morally wrong or right? Years ago, for example, most Americans were not pro-abortion (or even "pro-choice") and did not want abortion legalized. But a moral absolute regarding the sanctity of life has been dramatically tossed aside in recent times, so much so that even politicians who might be morally conservative in many areas have now moved to a pro-choice position and will not raise an objection to a woman's "right to choose."

Over the years, as society's beliefs about absolute moral standards have changed concerning abortion and other issues, the laws have changed accordingly. So while the majority might agree on particular standards and laws today, they can be overturned by the next generation. What may appear to be absolute for one generation might not be absolute for another,

Increasingly, people are becoming more tolerant, not only of abortion but also of gay marriage. Given the abortion example above, what is to prevent a majority of society declaring one day that same-sex marriage is permissible? And then what about polygamy, or even pedophilia? Indeed, a shifting morality can be a slippery slope, to the point that one day society might determine that polygamy and sex between adults and children are not wrong—as long as most people believe that they are acceptable. Now, some might object and say that these now-illegal things would never be allowed in America. But who in the 1960s would have believed that America would one day allow abortions and see gay marriages performed?

Without an absolute moral standard, people are free to make up their own morals (and change them as the majority dictates). Should we be surprised when some Western nations will one day allow parents to kill their newborns because there might be a defect in the child? The majority might be lulled into sympathizing with the anguished parent, and also piously thinking something like: "Who wants to have a child go through life in that kind of condition?"

DOES THE CHURCH HAVE THE ANSWER?

The gay marriage issue has been headline news across North America and on other continents. Even the acceptance of gay clergy has been widely noted in both secular and Christian media outlets.

- In November 2003 a part of the Episcopal Church voted to ordain a gay bishop. Thus, the world saw part of the church now condoning homosexual behavior.[3]

- On March 18, 2004, the Pacific Northwest Conference of the United Methodist Church in America supported a lesbian pastor. Once again, the world looked on as a large denomination legitimized homosexual behavior.[4]

[3] Episcopal Church consecrates openly gay bishop, CNN.com, November 3, 2003.
[4] Read the church proceedings for and against Rev. Karen Dammann at www.pnwumc.org/Dammann.htm.

As part of the public debate on the gay marriage issue, many church leaders have been interviewed on national TV programs and asked to share their position on this topic. While the majority of church leaders have been speaking against gay unions and have been defending marriage as being between one man and one woman, many of these same church leaders have not been able to adequately defend their position.

One Christian leader was interviewed on MSNBC-TV and was asked about the gay marriage issue. The interview went something like this:

> **TV host:** "Did Jesus deal directly with the gay marriage issue?"
>
> **Christian leader:** "No, but then Jesus didn't deal directly with the abortion issue or many other issues … ."

This is such a disappointing response. A proper response could have been such a powerful witness—not only to the interviewer but to the potential millions of viewers watching the news program, so people could understand why this Christian leader opposed gay marriage.

The same Christian leader appeared on CNN-TV doing an interview that, in part, went something like the following:

> **Interviewer:** "Why are you against gay marriage?"
>
> **Christian leader:** "Because down through the ages, culture after culture has taught that marriage is between a man and a woman."

We believe this kind of answer actually opens the door to gay marriage! How? Because it basically says that marriage is determined by law or opinion.

So, why is it that we don't see many Christian leaders giving the right sorts of answers? We think it's because the majority of them have compromised with the idea of millions of years of history, as well as evolutionary beliefs in astronomy, geology and so on. As a result, the Bible's authority has been undermined, and it's no longer understood to be the absolute authority.[5]

GAY MARRIAGE—IS EVOLUTION THE CAUSE?

After reading explanations from *Answers in Genesis* such as those above, some critics have concluded that we are saying that belief in millions of years or other evolutionary ideas is the cause of social ills like gay marriage. This is not true at all.

It is accurate to say that the increasing acceptance of homosexual behavior and gay marriage has gone hand in hand with the popularity and acceptance of millions of years and evolution-

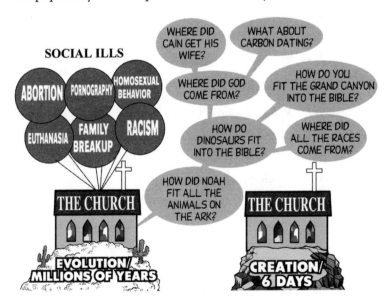

---

[5] For more information on this important point, see chapter 7: "Where did the idea of 'millions of years' come from?"

ary ideas. But this does not mean that every person who believes in millions of years/evolution accepts gay marriage or condones homosexual behavior.

But the more people (whether Christian or not) believe in man's ideas concerning the history of the universe, the more man's fallible ideas are used as a basis for determining "truth" and overriding the Bible's authority.

People need to understand that homosexual behavior and the gay marriage controversy are ultimately not the problems in our culture, but are the *symptoms* of a much deeper problem. Even though it's obvious from the Bible that homosexual behavior and gay marriage are an abomination (Romans 1 and other passages make this very clear), there is a foundational reason as to why there is an increasing acceptance of these ills in America and societies like it.

> What does the Bible say about homosexual behavior and gay marriage? Study the following verses:
> Genesis 2:18–25; Leviticus 18:22; Mark 10:6; Romans 1:26–27; 1 Corinthians 6:9–10; 1 Timothy 1:9–10

Cultures in the West were once pervaded by a primarily Christian worldview because the majority of people at least respected the Bible as the authority on morality.

It needs to be clearly understood that over the past two hundred years the Bible's authority has been increasingly undermined, as much of the church has compromised with the idea of millions of years (this began before Darwin) and has thus begun reinterpreting Genesis. When those outside the church saw church leaders rejecting Genesis as literal history, one can understand why they would have quickly lost respect for all of the Bible. If the church doesn't even believe this Book to be true, then why should the world build its morality on a fallible work that modern science supposedly has shown to be inaccurate in its science and history?

The Bible has lost respect in people's eyes (both within and without the church) to the extent that the culture as a whole now does not take the Bible's morality seriously at all. The increasing acceptance of homosexual behavior and gay marriage is a symptom of the loss of biblical authority, and is primarily due to the compromise the church has made with the secular world's teaching on origins.

MOCKING THE BIBLE

For example, consider the following. A New Orleans newspaper printed a commentary entitled, "In gay rights debate, Genesis is losing."[6] The column pointed out (correctly) that God intended marriage to be between one man and one woman. The writer even quoted Genesis 2:24, which declares, "Therefore shall a man leave his father and his mother and shall cleave to his wife: and they shall be one flesh."

The author then, mockingly, wrote, "Ah, Genesis. Heaven and earth created in six days, a serpent that talks and a 600-year-old man building an ark. Just the guide we need to set rational policy."

This secular writer recognized that the literal history of Genesis was the basis for the belief that marriage is one man for one woman. However, by mocking the Genesis account (just as many church leaders effectively do when they reinterpret Genesis 1–11 on the basis of man's fallible ideas), the writer removed the foundations

---

[6] Gill, J., *Times-Picayune*, New Orleans, March 5, 2004.

upon which the institution of marriage stands. This opens the door to gay marriage or anything else one might determine about marriage.

ARE PEOPLE BORN TO A HOMOSEXUAL LIFESTYLE?

We won't presume to offer a definitive answer as to what causes homosexual behavior. We can point out, however, that in a world that has experienced over 6,000 years of the Curse (Genesis 3), it is not difficult to argue that genetic factors accumulated over the millennia could lead to a predisposition toward aberrant behavior. And, of course, there is the combined factor of personal choice involved, where people who are inclined toward a certain behavior can decide whether or not to follow through on a course of action. In other words, a person's lifestyle can be influenced by

that individual's genetic makeup (and perhaps even by how that person was brought up—nature plus nurture).

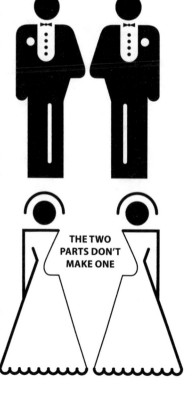

THE TWO
PARTS DON'T
MAKE ONE

In fact, Christian behavioral researchers point out, for example, that some people can be more genetically predisposed to alcoholism, to committing violent acts, etc. Now, this does not mean that these actions are to be condoned (the Bible calls them *sin*), because a predisposition does not lead a potential alcoholic to automatically walk into a bar to begin his drinking habit. Intentional, personal choice can certainly fend off that predisposition. While all people sin (Romans 3 and 6) and thus that is "natural," it does not make the sinning correct or acceptable.

Therefore, even if some genetic component (a so-called "homosexual gene" as some might call it) were found, it does not make this sin natural or normal. As indicated before, this world suffers from thousands of years of the Curse, and in this fallen, decaying world, all kinds of genetic mistakes have been occurring. It is important to note that such abnormalities are the result of the Curse, not of any creation by the Creator. Moreover, what Scripture teaches against certain behavior (drunkenness, infidelity, homosexual behavior, etc.,) trumps what anyone might say is acceptable behavior. There is right and wrong apart from people's opinions of what they might observe in nature and what it suggests to them, and that moral standard comes from God's Word.

It is possible that how a child grows up in certain situations might play a factor in determining sexual identity. Thankfully, though, the Bible presents all kinds of teaching on how to correctly raise children (see our book *The Genesis of a Legacy*). Sadly, though, it may not be far-fetched to say that as the breakdown of the family continues in America and as people increasingly reject biblical principles, impressionable young people will be even more inclined toward homosexuality, and thus gay marriage will probably grow. However, standing up for biblical truths in the culture can stem that tide.

GAY MARRIAGE—WHAT IS THE ANSWER?

In the Bible's book of Judges 17:6, we read this statement: "When they had no king to tell them what to do, they all did what was right in their own eyes." In other words, when there's no absolute authority to decide right and wrong, everyone has their own opinion as to what they should do.

So how could the Christian leader whose interviews were quoted earlier in this chapter have responded differently? Well, consider this answer:

> First of all, Jesus (who created us and therefore owns us and has the authority to determine right and wrong), as the God-man, *did* deal directly with the gay marriage issue, in the Bible's New Testament, in Matthew 19:4–6:

> "And He answered and said to them, 'Have you not read that He who made them at the beginning "made them male and female," and said, "For this reason a man shall leave his father and mother and be joined to his wife, and the two shall become one flesh?" So then, they are no longer two but one flesh. Therefore what God has joined together, let not man separate.' "

He could have continued:

> Christ quoted directly from the book of Genesis (and its account of the creation of Adam and Eve as the first man and woman—the first marriage) as literal history, to explain the doctrine of marriage as being one man for one woman. Thus marriage cannot be a man and a man, or a woman and a woman.

> Because Genesis is real history (as can be confirmed by observational science, incidentally),

Jesus dealt quite directly with the gay marriage issue when he explained the doctrine of marriage.

Not only this, but in John 1, we read:

"In the beginning was the Word, and the Word was with God, and the Word was God. The same was in the beginning with God. All things were made by him; and without him was not any thing made that was made."

Jesus, the Creator, is the Word. The Bible is the written Word. Every word in the Bible is really the Word of the Creator—Jesus Christ.[7]

Therefore, in Leviticus 18:22, Jesus deals directly with the homosexual issue, and thus the gay marriage issue. This is also true of Romans 1:26–27 and 1 Timothy 1:9–10.

Because Jesus in a real sense wrote all of the Bible, whenever Scripture deals with marriage and/or the homosexual issue, Jesus Himself is directly dealing with these issues.

Even in a secular context, the only answer a Christian should offer is this:

The Bible is the Word of our Creator, and Genesis is literal history. Its science and history can be trusted. Therefore, we have an absolute authority that determines marriage.

[7] See Colossians 1:15–20 as well.

God made the first man and woman—the first marriage. Thus, marriage can only be a man and a woman because we are accountable to the One who made marriage in the first place.

And don't forget—according to Scripture, one of the primary reasons for marriage is to produce godly offspring.[8] Adam and Eve were told to be fruitful and multiply, but there's no way a gay marriage can fulfill this command!

The battle against gay marriage will ultimately be lost (like the battle against abortion) *unless* the church and the culture return to the absolute authority beginning in Genesis. Then and only then will there be a true foundation for the correct doctrine of marriage—one man for one woman for life.

---

[8] Malachi 2:15: "Has not the Lord made them one? In flesh and spirit they are his. And why one? Because he was seeking godly offspring. So guard yourself in your spirit, and do not break faith with the wife of your youth."

WHAT'S THE BEST "PROOF" OF CREATION?

KEN HAM

If the Bible's account of creation is true, you may ask, then what's the best proof I can give to someone? Why doesn't all the evidence for creation convince scientists that evolution is wrong? Well, it's not that simple. In this chapter, we will examine the presuppositions that all people have and how this affects their interpretation of the evidence. We need to help evolutionists understand their own naturalistic presuppositions and see that the same "evidence" fits very nicely—in fact, even better—within a biblical worldview.

I N THIS ONGOING WAR BETWEEN creation and evolution, Christians are always looking for the strongest evidence for creation. They are looking for the "magic bullet" that will prove to their evolutionist friends that creation is true and evolution is false. This craving for evidence has led some Christians to be drawn to what we might call "flaky evidence." Over the past several years, some so-called "evidence" for creation has been shown not to be reliable. Some of these are

- supposed human and dinosaur footprints found together at the Paluxy River in Texas.

- the small accumulation of moon dust found by the Apollo astronauts.

- a boat-like structure in the Ararat region as evidence of Noah's Ark.

- a supposed human hand print found in "dinosaur-age rock."

- a dead "plesiosaur" caught near New Zealand.

Most well-meaning, informed creationists would agree in principle that things which are not carefully documented and researched should not be used. But in practice, many of them are very quick to accept the sorts of evidences mentioned here, without asking too many questions. They are less cautious than they might otherwise be, because they are so keen to have "our" facts/evidences to counter "theirs." What they really don't understand, however, is that it's not a matter of "their evidence vs. ours." *All* evidence is actually interpreted, and *all* scientists actually have the *same* observations—the same data—available to them.

EVIDENCE

Creationists and evolutionists, Christians and non-Christians, all have the *same* evidence—the same facts. Think about it: we all have the same earth, the same fossil layers, the same animals and plants, the same stars—the facts are all the same.

The difference is in the way we all *interpret* the facts. And why do we interpret facts differently? Because we start with different *presuppositions*; these are things that are assumed to be true without being able to prove them. These then become the basis

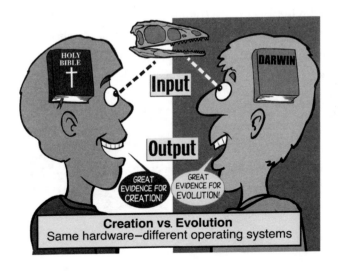

Creation vs. Evolution
Same hardware—different operating systems

for other conclusions. *All* reasoning is based on presuppositions (also called *axioms*). This becomes especially relevant when dealing with past events.

PAST AND PRESENT

We all exist in the present; and the facts all exist in the present. When one is trying to understand how the evidence came about (where did the animals come from? how did the fossil layers form? etc.), what we are actually trying to do is to connect the past to the present. However, if we weren't there in the past to observe events, how can we know what happened so that we can explain the present? It would be great to have a time machine so that we could know for sure about past events.

Christians, of course, claim they do have, in a sense, a time machine. They have a book called the Bible, which claims to be the Word of God who has always been there and has revealed to us the major events of the past about which we need to know. On the basis of these events (Creation, Fall, Flood, Babel, etc.), we have a set of presuppositions to build a way of thinking which enables us to interpret the evidence of the present.[1]

Evolutionists have certain beliefs about the past/present that they presuppose, e.g., no God (or at least none who performed acts of special creation); so they build a different way of thinking to interpret the evidence of the present.

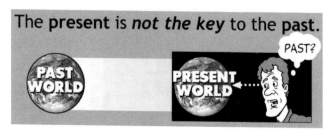

The **present** is *not the key* to the **past.**

---

[1] See chapter 13 on "What is a biblical worldview?" for further development of this idea.

Thus, when Christians and non-Christians argue about the evidence, in reality they are arguing about their *interpretations* based on their *presuppositions*.

That's why the argument often turns into something like:

"Can't you see what I'm talking about?"

"No, I can't. Don't you see how wrong you are?"

"No, I'm not wrong. It's obvious that I'm right."

"No, it's not obvious."

And so on.

These two people are arguing about the same evidence, but they are looking at the evidence through different glasses.

It's not until these two people recognize the argument is really about the presuppositions they have to start with, that they will begin to deal with the foundational reasons for their different beliefs. A person will not interpret the evidence differently until they put on a different set of glasses—which means to change one's presuppositions.

A Christian who understands these things can actually put on the evolutionist's glasses (without accepting the presuppositions as true) and understand how they look at evidence. However, for a number of reasons, including spiritual ones, a non-Christian usually can't put on the Christian's glasses—unless they recognize the presuppositional nature of the battle and are thus beginning to question their own presuppositions.

It is, of course, sometimes possible that just by presenting "evidence" one can convince a person that a particular scientific argument for creation makes sense of "the facts." But usually, if that person then hears a different *interpretation* of the same evidence that seems better than the first, that person will swing away from the first argument, thinking they have found "stronger facts."

However, if that person had been helped to understand this issue of presuppositions, then they would have been better able to recognize this for what it is—a different interpretation based on differing presuppositions (i.e., starting beliefs).

DEBATE TERMS

Often people who don't believe the Bible will say that they aren't interested in hearing about the Bible. They want real proof that there's a God who created. They'll listen to our claims about Christianity, but they want proof *without mentioning the Bible*.

If one agrees to a discussion without using the Bible as these people insist, then we have allowed *them* to set the terms of the debate. In essence these terms are:

1. **"Facts" are neutral.** However, there are no such things as "brute facts"; *all* facts are interpreted. Once the Bible is eliminated from the argument, the Christians' presuppositions are gone, leaving them unable to effectively give an alternate interpretation of the facts. Their opponents then have the upper hand as they still have *their* presuppositions.

2. **Truth can/should be determined independent of God.** However, the Bible states: "The fear of the Lord is the beginning of wisdom" (Psalm

CREATIONWISE   Dan Lietha

It would be foolish	for a soldier	to remove his armor and weapons	before a battle.	...NEXT, THROW DOWN YOUR SWORD! / OK	SURE, WE CAN TALK ABOUT EARTH'S ORIGINS, BUT LET'S LEAVE THE BIBLE OUT OF IT. / OK, NO PROBLEM!
Ephesians 6:10-17				**FOOLISH!**	**FOOLISH!**

111:10); "the fear of the Lord is the beginning of knowledge" (Proverbs 1:7); "but the natural man does not receive the things of the Spirit of God, for they are foolishness to him; neither can he know them, because they are spiritually discerned" (1 Corinthians 2:14).

A Christian cannot divorce the spiritual nature of the battle from the battle itself. A non-Christian is *not* neutral. The Bible makes this very clear: "The one who is not with Me is against Me, and the one who does not gather with Me scatters" (Matthew 12:30); "And this is the condemnation, that the Light has come into the world, and men loved darkness rather than the Light, because their deeds were evil" (John 3:19).

Agreeing to such terms of debate also implicitly accepts their proposition that the Bible's account of the universe's history is irrelevant to understanding that history!

ULTIMATELY, GOD'S WORD CONVICTS

1 Peter 3:15 and other passages make it clear we are to use every argument we can to convince people of the truth, and 2 Corinthians 10:4–5 says we are to refute error (as Paul did in his ministry to the Gentiles). Nonetheless, we must never forget

Revelation is *the key* to the past and the present!

Hebrews 4:12: "For the word of God is living and powerful and sharper than any two-edged sword, piercing even to the dividing apart of soul and spirit, and of the joints and marrow, and is a discerner of the thoughts and intents of the heart."

Also, Isaiah 55:11: "So shall My word be, which goes out of My mouth; it shall not return to Me void, but it shall accomplish what I please, and it shall certainly do what I sent it to do."

Even though our human arguments may be powerful, ultimately it is God's Word that convicts and opens people to the truth. In all of our arguments, we must not divorce what we are saying from the Word that convicts.

PRACTICAL APPLICATION

When someone says they want "proof" or "evidence," not the Bible, one might respond as follows:

> You might not believe the Bible, but I do. And I believe it gives me the right basis to understand this universe and correctly interpret the facts around me. I'm going to give you some examples of how building my thinking on the Bible explains the world and is not contradicted by science.

One can of course do this with numerous scientific examples, showing, for example, how the issue of sin and judgment is relevant to geology and fossil evidence; how the Fall of man, with the subsequent Curse on creation, makes sense of the evidence of harmful mutations, violence and death; or how the original "kinds" of animals gave rise to the wide variety of animals we see today.

Choose a topic and develop it:

> For instance, the Bible states that God made distinct *kinds* of animals and plants. Let me show

you what happens when I build my thinking on this presupposition. I will illustrate how processes such as natural selection, genetic drift, etc. can be explained and interpreted. You will see how the science of genetics makes sense based upon the Bible. Evolutionists believe in natural selection—that is real science, as you observe it happening. Well, creationists also believe in natural selection. Evolutionists accept the science of genetics—well, so do creationists.

However, here is the difference: evolutionists believe that, over millions of years, one kind of animal has changed into a totally different kind. However, creationists, based on the Bible's account of origins, believe that God created separate kinds of animals and plants to reproduce their own kind; therefore, one kind will not turn into a totally different kind.

Now this can be tested in the present. The scientific observations support the creationist interpretation that the changes we see are not creating new information. The changes are all within the originally created pool of information of that kind—sorting, shuffling or degrading it. The creationist account of history, based on the Bible, provides the correct basis to interpret the evidence of the present; and real science confirms the interpretation.

After this detailed explanation, continue:

Now let me ask you to defend *your* position concerning these matters. Please show me how *your* way of thinking, based on *your* beliefs, makes sense of the same evidence. And I want you to point out where my science and logic are wrong.

In arguing this way, a Christian is

1. using biblical presuppositions to build a way of thinking to interpret the evidence.

2. showing that the Bible and science go hand in hand.

3. challenging the presuppositions of the other person (many are unaware they have these).

4. forcing the debater to logically defend his position consistent with science and his own presuppositions (many will find that they cannot do this).

5. honoring the Word of God that convicts the soul.

If Christians really understood that all evidence is actually interpreted on the basis of certain presuppositions, we wouldn't be in the least bit intimidated by the evolutionists' supposed "evidence." We should instead be looking at the evolutionists' (or old-earthers'[2]) *interpretation* of the evidence, and how the same evidence could be interpreted within a biblical framework and confirmed by testable and repeatable science. If more creationists did this, they would be less likely to jump at flaky evidence that seems startling but in reality has been interpreted incorrectly in their rush to find the knockdown, drag-out convincing "evidence"

---

[2] Those who accept millions of years of history.

against evolution that they think they desperately need.

The various age-dating methods are also subject to interpretation. All dating methods suffer, in principle, from the same limitations—whether they are used to support a young world or an old world. For instance, the public reads almost daily in newspapers and magazines that scientists have dated a particular rock at billions of years old. Most just accept this. However, creation scientists have learned to ask questions as to how this date was obtained—what method was used and what *assumptions* were accepted to develop this method? These scientists then question those assumptions (questions) to see whether they are valid and to determine whether the rock's age could be interpreted differently. Then the results are published to help people understand that scientists have not proven that the rock is billions of years old and that the evidence can be interpreted in a different way to support a young age.

Consider the research from the creationist RATE group (Radioisotopes and the Age of The Earth) concerning the age of zircon crystals in granite.[3] Using one set of assumptions, these crystals could be interpreted to be around 1.5 billion years old based on the amount of lead produced from the decay of uranium (which also produces helium). However, if one questions these assumptions, one is motivated to test them. Measurements of the rate at which helium is able to "leak out" of these crystals indicate that if they were much older than about 6,000 years, they would have nowhere near the amount of helium still left in them. Hence, the originally applied assumption of a constant decay rate is flawed; one must assume, instead, that there has been acceleration of the decay rate in the past. Using this revised assumption,

---

[3] Humphreys, R., *et. al.*, Helium diffusion rates support accelerated nuclear decay, www.icr.org/pdf/research/Helium_ICC_7-22-03.pdf.

the same uranium-lead data can now be interpreted to also give an age of fewer than 6,000 years.

Another example involves red blood cells and traces of hemoglobin that have been found in *T. rex* bones, although these should have long decomposed if they were millions of years old. Yet the reaction of the researchers was a perfect illustration of how evolutionary bias can result in trying to explain away hard facts to fit the preconceived framework of millions of years:

> It was exactly like looking at a slice of modern bone. But, of course, I couldn't believe it. I said to the lab technician: "The bones, after all, are 65 million years old. How could blood cells survive that long?"[4]

Whenever you hear a news report that scientists have found another "missing link" or discovered a fossil "millions of years old," try to think about the right questions that need to be asked to challenge the questions these scientists asked to get their interpretations!

All of this should be a lesson for us to take note of the situation when we read the newspaper—we are reading someone's interpretation of the facts of world history—there very well could be a different way of looking at the same "facts." One can see this in practice on television when comparing a news network that's currently considered fairly liberal (CNN) with one that is more conservative (FOX)—one can often see the same "facts" interpreted differently!

The reason so many Christian professors (and Christian leaders in general) have rejected the literal creation position is that they have blindly accepted the interpretation of evidence from

---

4   *Science* **261**:160, July 9, 1994; see also Scientists recover *T. rex* soft tissue: 70-million-year-old fossil yields preserved blood vessels, www.msnbc.msn.com/id/7285683/, March 24, 2005.

the secular world, based on man's fallible presuppositions about history. And they have then tried to reinterpret the Bible accordingly. If only they would start with the presupposition that God's Word is true, they would find that they could then correctly interpret the evidence of the present and show overwhelmingly that observational science repeatedly confirms such interpretations.

And don't forget, as Christians, we need to always build our thinking on the Word of the One who has the answers to all of the questions that could ever be asked—the infinite Creator God. He has revealed the true history of the universe in His Word to enable us to develop the right way of thinking about the present and thus determine the correct interpretations of the evidence of the present. We should follow Proverbs 1:7 and 9:10, which teach that fear of the Lord is the beginning of true wisdom and knowledge.

THE BOTTOM LINE

The bottom line is that it's not a matter of who has the better (or the most) "facts on their side." We need to understand that there are no such things as brute facts—*all* facts are interpreted. The next time evolutionists use what seem to be convincing facts

Secular history   Biblical history

for evolution, try to determine the *presuppositions* they have used to interpret these facts. Then, beginning with the big picture of history from the Bible, look at the same facts through these biblical glasses and interpret them differently. Next, using the real science of the present that an evolutionist also uses, see if that science, when properly understood, confirms (by being consistent with) the interpretation based on the Bible. You will find over and over again that the Bible is confirmed by real science.

But remember that, like Job (42:2–6), we need to understand that compared to God we know next to nothing. We won't have all the answers. However, so many answers have come to light now that a Christian can give a credible defense of the book of Genesis and show it is the correct foundation for thinking about, and interpreting, every aspect of reality.

Therefore, let's not jump in a blind-faith way at the startling evidences we think we need to "prove" creation—trying to counter "their facts" with "our facts." (Jesus Himself rose from the dead in the most startling possible demonstration of the truth of God's Word. But many still wouldn't believe—cf. Luke 16:27–31.) Instead, let's not let apparent evidences for evolution intimidate us, but let's understand the right way to think about evidence. We can then deal with *the same evidence the evolutionists use*, to show they have the wrong framework of interpretation—and that the facts of the real world really do conform to, and confirm, the Bible. In this way we can do battle for a biblical worldview.

And remember, it's no good convincing people to believe in creation, without also leading them to believe and trust in the Creator and Redeemer, Jesus Christ. God honors those who honor His Word. We need to use God-honoring ways of reaching people with the truth of what life is all about.

WHAT IS A BIBLICAL BIBLICAL WORLDVIEW?

STACIA MCKEEVER

Our goal in this book has been to provide logical answers to much of what the media and the educational system throw at us concerning evolution and origins. We want to help all Christians think biblically and critically about the messages they hear. The Bible gives us the true history of the universe, and it is only in light of that history that we can interpret the evidence of the present, explain death and suffering or offer true answers for the problems of mankind. In this chapter, we want to retrace that history, which gives us the foundation for a truly biblical worldview that allows us to explain all that we see.

THE HISTORY AS RECORDED IN the Bible has been attacked by our increasingly secular culture. As a result, recent generations have been brought up to see the Bible as a book that contains many interesting stories and religious teaching but has no connection to reality.

This limited viewpoint helps explain why there are so many questions about how the Bible can explain dinosaurs, fossils, death and suffering and many other topics that relate to our real world.

This chapter will outline the major events of the past (and even the future)—the "7 C's of History"—that are foundational to the Bible's important message and demonstrate how the Bible connects to the real world.

CREATION

God created the heavens, the earth and all that is in them in six normal-length days around 6,000 years ago. His completed *creation* was "very good" (Genesis 1:31), and all the original animals (including dinosaurs) and the first two humans (Adam and Eve) ate only plants (Genesis 1:29–30). Life was perfect and not yet affected by the Curse—death, violence, disease, sickness, thorns and fear had no part in the original creation.

After He was finished creating, God "rested" (or stopped) from His work, although He continues to uphold the creation (Colossians 1:17). His creation of all things in six days and resting on the seventh set a pattern for our week, which He designed for us to follow.

The science of "information theory" confirms that first statement of the Bible, "In the beginning God created ... ." DNA is the molecule of heredity, part of a staggeringly complex system, more information-dense than that in the most efficient supercomputer. Since the information in our DNA can only come from a source of greater information (or intelligence), there must have been something other than matter in the beginning. This other source must have no limit to its intelligence; in fact, it must be an ultimate source of intelligence from which all things have come. The Bible tells us there is such a source—God. Since God has no beginning and no end and knows all (Psalm 147:5), it makes sense that God is the source of the information we see all around us! This fits with real science, just as we would expect.[1]

In Genesis, God explains that He created things to reproduce after their "kinds." And this is what we observe today: great variation within different "kinds" (e.g., dogs, cats, elephants, etc.), but not one kind changing into another, as molecules-to-man evolution requires.[2]

CORRUPTION

After God completed His perfect creation, He told Adam that he could eat from any tree in the Garden of Eden (Genesis 2:8) except one—the Tree of the Knowledge of Good and Evil. He warned Adam that death would be the punishment for disobedience (Genesis 2:17). Instead of listening to the command of his Creator, Adam chose to rebel, eating the fruit from the tree (Genesis 3:6). Because our holy God must punish sin, He sacrificed animals to make coverings for Adam and Eve, and He sent the first couple from the garden, mercifully denying them access to the Tree of Life so that they would not live forever in their sinful state.

---

1   For a more in-depth analysis of the complexity of DNA and information theory, see www.AnswersInGenesis.org/infotheory.

2   For more information, see www.AnswersInGenesis.org/liger.

Adam's sin ushered death, sickness and sorrow into the once-perfect creation (Genesis 3:19; Romans 5:12). God also pronounced a curse on the world, changing it completely (Genesis 3; Romans 8:20–22). As a result, the world that we now live in is merely a decaying remnant—a *corruption*—of the beautiful, righteous world that Adam and Eve originally called home. We see the results of this corruption all around us in the form of carnivorous animals, mutations, sickness, disease and death.[3] The good news is that, rather than leave His precious handiwork without hope, God graciously promised to one day send a Redeemer who would buy back His people from the curse of sin (Genesis 3:15).

CATASTROPHE

As the descendants of Adam and Eve married and filled the earth with offspring, their wickedness was great (Genesis 6:5). God judged their sin by sending a global Flood to destroy all men, animals, creatures that moved along the ground, and birds of the air (Genesis 6:7). Those God chose to enter the Ark—Noah, his family and land-dwelling representatives of the animal kingdom (including dinosaurs)—were saved from the watery *catastrophe*.

There was plenty of room in the huge vessel for tens of thousands of animals—even dinosaurs (the average dinosaur was only the size of a sheep, and Noah didn't have to take fully grown adults of the large dinosaurs). Noah actually needed only about 16,000 animals on the Ark to represent all the distinct kinds of land-dwelling animals.[4]

---

[3]   For more information, see www.AnswersInGenesis.org/curse.

[4]   See *Noah's Ark: A Feasibility Study* by John Woodmorappe for a detailed analysis of the capacity of this huge ship to hold all the residents of the Ark.

This earth-covering event has left its mark even today. From the thousands of feet of sedimentary rock found around the world to the "billions of dead things buried in rock layers" (fossils), the Flood reminds us even today that our righteous God cannot—and will not—tolerate sin, while the Ark reminds us that He provides a way of salvation from sin's punishment. The rainbows we experience today remind us of God's promise never again to destroy the earth with water (Genesis 9:13–15). Incidentally, if the flood were a local event (rather than global in extent), as some claim, then God has repeatedly broken His promise since we continue to experience local flooding even today.[5]

CONFUSION

After the Flood, God commanded Noah and his family—the only humans left in the world—and the animals to fill the earth (Genesis 8:17). However, the human race once again disobeyed God's command and built a tower, which they hoped would keep them together (Genesis 11:3–4). So, around 100 years after the Flood waters had retreated, God brought a *confusion* (a multiplicity) of languages in place of the common language the people shared, causing them to spread out over the earth. The several different languages created suddenly at Babel (Genesis 10–11) could each subsequently give rise to many more. Languages gradually change; so when a group of people breaks up into several groups that no longer interact, after a few centuries they may each speak a different (but related) language. Today, we have thousands of languages but fewer than twenty language "families."[6]

All the tribes and nations in the world today have descended

5   For more information, see www.AnswersInGenesis.org/flood.
6   For more information, see www.AnswersInGenesis.org/linguistics.

from these various groups. Despite what you may have been led to believe about our seeming superficial differences, we really are all "one blood" (Acts 17:26)—descendants of Adam and Eve through Noah and his family—and all, therefore, are in need of salvation from sin.

God had created Adam and Eve with the ability to produce children with a variety of different characteristics. This ability was passed on through Noah and his family. As the people scattered, they took with them different amounts of genetic information for certain characteristics—e.g., height, the amount of pigment for hair and skin color (by the way, we all have the same pigment, just more or less of it) and so on.

In fact, the recent Human Genome Project supports this biblical teaching that there is only *one* biological race of humans. As one report says, "… it is clear that what is called 'race' … reflects just a few continuous traits determined by a tiny fraction of our genes."[7] The basic principles of genetics explain various shades of *one* skin color (not different colors) and how the distinct people groups (e.g., American Indians, Australian Aborigines) came about because of the event at the Tower of Babel. The creation and Flood legends of these peoples, from all around the world, also confirm the Bible's anthropology to be true.

CHRIST

God's perfect creation was corrupted by Adam when he disobeyed God, ushering sin and death into the world. Because of Adam's disobedience and because we have all sinned personally, we are all deserving of the death penalty and need a Savior (Romans 5:12).

7　Pääbo, S., The human genome and our view of ourselves, *Science* **291**(5507):1219–1220, 2001.

As mentioned before, God did not leave His precious—but corrupted—creation without hope. He promised to one day send Someone who would take away the penalty for sin, which is death (Genesis 3:15; Ezekiel 18:4; Romans 6:23).

God killed at least one animal in the Garden of Eden because of the sin of Adam; subsequently, Adam's descendants sacrificed animals. Such sacrifices could only cover sin—they pointed toward the time when the One whom God would send (Hebrews 9) would make the ultimate sacrifice.

When God gave Moses the Law, people began to see that they could never measure up to God's standard of perfection (Romans 3:20)—if they broke any part of the Law, the result was the same as breaking all of it (James 2:10). They needed Someone to take away their imperfection and present them faultless before God's throne (Romans 5:9; 1 Peter 3:18).

In line with God's purpose and plan for everything, He sent His promised Savior at just the right time (Galatians 4:4). There was a problem, however. All humans are descended from Adam and, therefore, all humans are born with sin. God's chosen One had to be perfect, as well as infinite, to take away the infinite penalty for sin.

God solved this "problem" by sending His Son, Jesus *Christ*—completely human and completely God. Think of it: the Creator of the universe (John 1:1–3, 14) became part of His creation so that He might save His people from their sins!

Jesus fulfilled more than fifty prophecies made about Him centuries before, showing He was the One promised over 4,000 years before by His Father (Genesis 3:15). While He spent over thirty years on Earth, He never once sinned—He did nothing wrong. He healed many people, fed huge crowds and taught thousands of listeners about their Creator God and how to be reconciled to Him. He even confirmed the truth of Genesis by explaining that marriage is between one man and one woman (Matthew 19:3–6, quoting Genesis 1:27 and 2:24).

CROSS

Jesus is called the "Last Adam" in 1 Corinthians 15:45. While Adam disobeyed God's command not to eat the forbidden fruit, Jesus fulfilled the Creator's purpose that He die for the sin of the world.

The first Adam brought death into the world through his disobedience; the Last Adam brought eternal life with God through His obedience (1 Corinthians 15:21–22).

Because God is perfectly holy, He must punish sin—either the sinner himself or a substitute to bear His wrath. Jesus bore God's wrath for our sin by dying in our place on the *Cross* (Isaiah 53:6). The Lamb of God (John 1:29; Revelation 5:12) was sacrificed once for all (Hebrews 7:27) so that all those who believe in Him will be saved from the ultimate penalty for sin (eternal separation from God) and will live with Him forever.

Jesus Christ, the Creator of all things (John 1:1–3; Colossians 1:15–16), was not defeated by death. He rose three days after He was crucified, showing that He has power over all things, including death, the "last enemy" (1 Corinthians 15:26). As Paul wrote, "O death, where is your sting? O grave, where is your victory? … But thanks be to God who gives us the victory through our Lord Jesus Christ" (1 Corinthians 15:55, 57).

When we believe in Christ and understand what He has done for us, we are passed from death into life (John 5:24). The names of those who receive Him are written in the Lamb's Book of Life (Revelation 13:8; 17:8)—when they die, they will go to be with Him forever (John 3:16).

Just as "science" cannot prove that Jesus rose from the dead, it cannot prove that God created everything in six days. In fact, "science" can't prove any event from history because it is limited in dealings about the past. Historical events are known to be true because of reliable eyewitness accounts. In fact, there are reliable eyewitness accounts that Jesus' tomb was empty after three days and that He later appeared to as many as 500 people at once (1 Corinthians 15:6). Of course, we know that both the Resurrection and creation in six days are true because God, who cannot lie, states in His Word that these things happened.

While the secular history of millions of years isn't true, and evolutionary geology, biology, anthropology, astronomy, etc., do not stand the test of observational science, the Bible's history, from Genesis 1 onward, *is* true; the Bible's geology, biology, anthropology, astronomy, etc., are confirmed by observational science. Therefore, the fact that the Bible's history is true should challenge people to seriously consider the Bible's message of salvation that is based in this history.

CONSUMMATION

Death has been around almost as long as humans have. Romans 8 tells us that the whole of creation is suffering because of Adam's sin. As terrible as things are, however, they are not a permanent part of creation.

God, in His great mercy, has promised not to leave His creation in its sinful state. He has promised to do away with the corruption that Adam brought into the world. He has promised to remove, in the future, the curse He placed on His creation (Revelation 22:3) and to make a new heaven and a new Earth (2 Peter 3:13). In this new place there will be no death, crying or pain

(Revelation 21:4).

Those who have repented and believed in what Jesus did for them on the Cross can look forward to the *consummation* of God's kingdom—this new heaven and Earth—knowing they will enjoy God forever in a wonderful place. In the future, God will take away the corruption that was introduced in the Garden of Eden, giving us once again a perfect place to live!

A worldview based on a proper understanding of the history of the world, as revealed in the Bible, is what every Christian needs to combat our society's evolutionary propaganda.

ABOUT THE AUTHORS

KEN HAM

Founder and CEO, Answers in Genesis–US

B.Sc., environmental biology, Queensland Institute of Technology; Dip. Ed., University of Queensland; Honorary Doctor of Divinity, Temple Baptist College; Honorary Doctorate in Literature, Liberty University

As founder and CEO of Answers in Genesis-US, Ken is one of America's most in-demand Christian speakers. He is the author of many books on Genesis, including the best-selling *The Lie: Evolution,* and a number of children's books (*Dinosaurs of Eden, D is for Dinosaur, A is for Adam,* etc.). Ken has also co-authored several books including *Darwin's Plantation* and *How Could a Loving God . . . ?*

Ken's bachelor's degree in applied science (with an emphasis on environmental biology) was awarded by the Queensland Institute of Technology in Australia. He also holds a diploma of education from the University of Queensland (a graduate qualification necessary for Ken to have begun his initial career as a science teacher in the public schools in Australia).

In recognition of the contribution Ken has made to the church in the USA and internationally, Ken has been awarded two honorary doctorates: a Doctor of Divinity (1997) from Temple Baptist College in Cincinnati, Ohio, and a Doctor of Literature (2004) from Liberty University in Lynchburg, Virginia.

Ken is heard daily on the radio feature *Answers ... with Ken Ham* (broadcast on more than 900 stations—and over 100 additional outlets—worldwide), and has appeared on national TV (e.g., *The NBC Nightly News with Brian Williams, The PBS News Hour with Jim Lehrer*) and talk-show programs. He also writes articles and helps edit AiG's *Answers* magazine.

Ken's teaching emphasis is on the relevance and authority of the book of Genesis in the life of the average Christian, and how compromise on Genesis has opened a dangerous door regarding how the culture and church view biblical authority. His Australian accent, keen sense of humor, captivating stories and exceptional PowerPoint illustrations have made him one of North America's most effective Christian communicators.

OTHER TITLES BY KEN HAM

The Lie: Evolution (Book)
Why Won't They Listen? (Book)
How Could a Loving God ... ? (Book)
Darwin's Plantation (Book with Dr. Charles Ware)
The Great Dinosaur Mystery Solved (Book)
Dinosaurs of Eden (Book)
Creation Mini Series with Ken Ham (DVD series)

See pages 185–186

BODIE HODGE

Speaker, writer, *Answers in Genesis*–US

B.S. and M.S., mechanical engineering, Southern Illinois University at Carbondale

Bodie went to Southern Illinois University at Carbondale (SIUC) and received a BS and MS in mechanical engineering. His specialty was a subset of mechanical engineering based in advanced materials processing, particularly starting powders.

Bodie did research for his master's degree through a grant from Lockheed Martin and developed a new method of production of submicron titanium diboride. The new process produced titanium diboride cheaper, faster and with higher quality. This technology is essential for some nanotechnologies.

Bodie worked as a mechanical engineer for *Grain Systems Incorporated*, a test engineer for *Aerotek Engineering* (working for *Caterpillar Inc.*) and taught undergraduate engineering courses at SIUC before joining *Answers in Genesis*.

Bodie is currently a speaker with Answers in Genesis–US and assists in development of web content and education resources.

CARL KERBY

International speaker, research and writer,
Answers in Genesis–US

Carl Kerby is a founding board member of Answers in Genesis–US and one of AiG's most dynamic lecturers on the book of Genesis.

Carl became a Christian in 1987 after attending a crusade in Salt Lake City, Utah. He grew up in a very liberal church and in a family that was involved in the wild world of professional wrestling. He had been taught that evolution could just be added to the Bible, but in the late 1980s a pilot challenged Carl on the creation/evolution issue. After personal Bible study and reading Ken Ham's book, *The Lie: Evolution*, Carl's faith was totally renewed. He now knew that God's Word is true from the beginning.

Carl served in the military for 8 years as an air traffic controller. He then worked for the FAA as an air traffic controller, spending the last 10 years of his career at Chicago's busy O'Hare International Airport. Carl joined AiG full-time in 2004.

OTHER TITLES BY CARL KERBY

Genesis: The Bottom Strip of the Christian Faith (DVD)
Racism—Is There an Answer? (DVD)
What Is the Best Evidence That God Created? (DVD)
Remote Control (Book)

See page 187

DR. JASON LISLE

Speaker, researcher and writer, Answers in Genesis–US

B.S., physics and astronomy, Ohio Wesleyan University; MS and Ph.D., astrophysics, University of Colorado at Boulder

Dr. Jason Lisle graduated *summa cum laude* from Ohio Wesleyan University where he double-majored in physics and astronomy. He earned his Master's degree and Ph.D. in astrophysics from the University of Colorado at Boulder. Jason's area of specialty in graduate school was solar astrophysics.

Dr. Lisle was raised in a Christian home, and because his family believed in the authority and accuracy of the Bible, he had little difficulty in dealing with the evolutionary bombardment he received in school. At the university, Jason discovered that scientists are usually not aware of their presuppositions, and when the evidence is properly interpreted, it always supports the biblical account of creation.

Dr. Lisle is now helping Answers in Genesis–US (and the creation movement as a whole) refute the evolutionary account of origins. He is also helping design exciting planetarium programs for the popular Creation Museum in Northern Kentucky (near Cincinnati, Ohio).

OTHER TITLES BY DR. JASON LISLE

Distant Starlight (DVD)

Creation Astronomy (DVD)

Dinosaurs and the Bible (DVD)

Creation: Science Confirms the Bible is True (DVD)

Created Cosmos (DVD)

Taking Back Astronomy (Book)   See page 187

STACIA MCKEEVER

Speaker, researcher and writer, Answers in Genesis–US

B.S., biology and B.A., psychology, Clearwater Christian College

Stacia graduated *summa cum laude* in biology and psychology from Clearwater Christian College. She has been working full-time for Answers in Genesis–US since 1997. Stacia has written or coauthored a number of articles for the AiG website (www. AnswersInGenesis.org).

Stacia has conducted hands-on workshops for young children around the US for several years and has written curricula (*Beginnings, Questions,* and *The Seven C's of History*) and workbooks for elementary-aged children. Stacia has written for *The Godly Business Woman* and *Evangelizing Today's Child,* and has researched and written copy for several Bible-themed calendars.

Stacia recently became a certified scuba-diver and enjoys traveling internationally. She and her husband Seth reside in southeastern Indiana.

OTHER TITLES BY STACIA MCKEEVER

Beginnings (Answers for Kids curriculum)
The Seven C's of History (Answers for Kids curriculum)
Questions (Answers for Kids curriculum)
Why is Keiko Sick? (Book)

See page 188

DR. DAVID MENTON

Speaker, researcher and writer, Answers in Genesis–US

B.A., Mankato State University; Ph.D., cell biology, Brown University

Now retired, Dr. Menton served as a biomedical research technician at Mayo Clinic and then as an associate professor of anatomy at Washington University School of Medicine (St. Louis) for more than 30 years. He was a consulting editor in histology for *Stedman's Medical Dictionary*, and has received numerous awards for his teaching.

Dr. Menton is a popular speaker for Answers in Genesis–US and has spoken throughout the US and Canada on the creation/evolution issue for nearly twenty years. He has been profiled in *American Men and Women of Science—A Biographical Directory of Today's Leaders in Physical, Biological and Related Sciences* for almost two decades.

OTHER TITLES BY DR. DAVID MENTON

The Evolutionary Controversy (DVD)
Fearfully and Wonderfully Made (DVD)
Dinosaurs by Design (DVD)
Lucy—She's No Lady! (DVD)
Inherently Wind: A Hollywood History of the Scopes Trial (DVD)
The Hearing Ear and the Seeing Eye (DVD)
Formed to Fly (DVD)

See page 189

DR. TERRY MORTENSON

Speaker, researcher and writer, Answers in Genesis–US

B.A., math, University of Minnesota; M. Div., Trinity Evangelical Divinity School; Ph.D., history of geology, Coventry University, England

Like most people, Terry Mortenson grew up in an education system that taught evolution as fact. During his first year at the University of Minnesota, and shortly after becoming a Christian, Terry began to see the fallacy of the idea of billions of years of evolution.

Terry worked with Campus Crusade for Christ (CCC) for 25 years. After 4 years of campus ministry, Terry and his wife Margie moved to Europe where Terry served as country director for Czechoslovakia. Terry and his family have lived in Austria, Hungary and England.

With an M. Div. from Trinity Evangelical Divinity School and a Ph.D. in the history of geology from Coventry University in England, Dr. Mortenson has been studying and speaking on the creation-evolution controversy throughout North America and Europe since the late 1970s. He has spoken to various kinds of audiences (young children, teens, university students, lay people, professors) in various settings (homes, churches, schools, university classrooms and public lecture halls) and in many countries (America, England, Russia and most countries of Eastern Europe).

OTHER TITLES BY DR. TERRY MORTENSON

The Origin of Old-Earth Geology & Christian Compromise
    in the Early 19th Century (2 DVDs)
Origin of the Species (DVD)
The Great Turning Point (Book)
Standing Against the Myth (audio CD set)
Noah's Flood (DVD) See page 188

DR. GEORGIA PURDOM

Speaker, researcher and writer, Answers in Genesis–US

B.A., biology, Cedarville University; Ph.D., molecular genetics, Ohio State University

Dr. Georgia Purdom received her Ph.D. in molecular genetics from Ohio State University in 2000. She is a member of the Human Anatomy and Physiology Society, American Society for Cell Biology, Creation Research Society and American Society for Microbiology.

Dr. Purdom has published papers in the *Journal of Neuroscience*, the *Journal of Bone and Mineral Research* and the *Journal of Leukocyte Biology*. Her particular area of interest is in the role of mutations and horizontal gene transfer in microbial populations (and other organisms) in natural selection.

Georgia is engaged in full-time research, writing, and speaking on the topic of creation for Answers in Genesis–US. Additionally, she helped to launch and teaches courses for AnswersOnline-Education.org, AiG's web-based curricula for youth and adults.

OTHER TITLES BY DR. GEORGIA PURDOM

The Intelligent Design Movement (DVD)

The Code of Life (DVD)

See page 190

MIKE RIDDLE

Speaker and writer, Answers in Genesis–US

B.S., mathematics, Colorado State University of Pueblo; M.Ed., Pepperdine University, Los Angeles, CA

Mike Riddle has led teaching seminars in creation education for over twenty years all over the world. He is a popular and dynamic speaker and is often the keynote speaker at large meetings, including various homeschool conventions.

Mike's accomplishments include national champion in track & field (pentathlon–1976), captain in the Marines and manager of Microsoft's worldwide technical training.

Mike joined the Answers in Genesis–US staff in January of 2005 as a full-time speaker and writer. Not only does he speak for AiG many times each year, but Mike also helps develop curriculum materials.

Mike currently resides in Northern Kentucky with his wife, and chief volunteer supporter, Lesley.

OTHER TITLES BY MIKE RIDDLE

Cloning, Stems Cells, & the Value of Life (DVD)
The Riddle of Origins (DVD set)
The Riddle of Dinosaurs (Kids DVD)

See page 190

INDEX

THE LIE: EVOLUTION BOOK

KEN HAM is best known for his message on the relevance of creation and the importance of Genesis. Humorous and easy to read, this book powerfully equips Christians to defend the Book of Genesis and opens eyes to the evil effects of evolution on today's society. *168 pages. (Jr. High–Adult)*

Study guide available!

THE GREAT DINOSAUR MYSTERY SOLVED! BOOK

KEN HAM explains how to understand Earth's history … from a biblical perspective, and then applies this biblical foundation to the intriguing topic of dinosaurs. The Bible actually makes dinosaurs come "alive" as their great mystery is solved. *189 pages. (Jr. High–Adult)*

Study guide available!

WHY WON'T THEY LISTEN? BOOK

KEN HAM • This revolutionary book has already opened the eyes of thousands of Christians, showing why the traditional methods of evangelism are not reaching today's humanistic, evolutionized culture. By applying proven soul-winning methods as found in the Scriptures, this book will revolutionize your witnessing. *181 pages. (High School–Adult)*

Study guide available!

HOW COULD A LOVING GOD . . . ? BOOK

KEN HAM • When hard times hit, even seasoned Christians find themselves asking, "Why?" With sensitivity to the person whose perception of God has been calloused by tragedy, apologist/Bible teacher Ken Ham makes clear the hope-giving answers found in the pages of Scripture. *208 pages. (High School–Adult)*

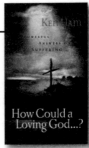

DARWIN'S PLANTATION BOOK

KEN HAM & DR. CHARLES WARE • Most people do not realize how intimately connected the idea of evolution and the worst racist ideology in history are. This fascinating book gives a compelling history of the effect of evolution on the history of the United States, including slavery and the civil rights movement. *192 pages. (Jr. High–Adult)*

For more information visit answersingenesis.org
or visit your local bookseller.

DINOSAURS OF EDEN BOOK

KEN HAM • Follow two young people who travel through time, discovering facts about dinosaurs in many eras. Scripture and historical information are intertwined to present a fascinating account of history from the creation to the Judgment, by way of salvation through Jesus Christ. Wonderfully illustrated. *64 pages. Hardcover. (Age 10–Adult)*

A IS FOR ADAM BOOK

KEN & MALLY HAM present the gospel in rhyme. ABC rhymes with full-color illustrations make this teaching book fun and exciting for kids of all ages. In the back of this book you'll find explanatory notes and creative ways to teach and explain the gospel to your children. *20 pages. (Pre-reader–Adult)*

D IS FOR DINOSAUR BOOK

KEN & MALLY HAM • It's a rhyme/alphabet/coloring book for the whole family, teaching about creation, the Fall, the Flood, salvation, the gospel, dinosaurs and fossils. Thirty full-color illustrations. *123 pages. (Pre-reader–Adult)*

MY CREATION BIBLE BOOK

KEN HAM, writes in delightful verse, and explains difficult passages in a thoughtful way. Teaching young minds that early Genesis is not only real history, but a look forward to God's beautiful restoration, Brings the Bible to life. *Free music CD (Ages 2–6)*

DINOSAURS, GENESIS & THE GOSPEL DVD

BUDDY DAVIS AND KEN HAM • This upbeat educational video is packed with music and fun biblical teaching. Ken and Buddy answer common dinosaurs questions that relate to the Bible. A free Discussion Guide is also included. *2 DVDs and Discussion Guide. 2 parts, approximately 30 minutes each. (Preschool-Grade 6)*

For more information visit answersingenesis.org or visit your local bookseller.

GENESIS: THE "BOTTOM STRIP" OF THE CHRISTIAN FAITH DVD

CARL KERBY • The former air traffic controller explains the importance of following the "bottom strip" if you are to find happiness and purpose in life. You don't have to be a "professional" Christian to be effective in your service to God. *49 minutes. (High School–Adult)*

RACISM—IS THERE AN ANSWER? DVD

CARL KERBY • Searching for answers to one of the greatest challenges of our day? Carl Kerby sheds light from God's Word and from real science on the truth about so-called "races": we all share a common ancestor in Adam! *45 minutes. (High School–Adult)*

WHAT IS THE BEST EVIDENCE THAT GOD CREATED? DVD

CARL KERBY • Audiences nationwide have been thrilled with this colorful, eye-catching presentation on some of the most astounding evidences of God's handiwork. The talk builds to an unforgettable conclusion: the life-changing truth that the best evidence is God's Word itself! *45 minutes. (High School–Adult)*

CREATED COSMOS CREATION MUSEUM DVD

DR. JASON LISLE combines eye-popping images and animation with faith-affirming facts from science and Scripture in this awe-inspiring planetarium show. The result is that a difficult message—the immense size and scale of the universe—is made simple! *22 minutes (Jr. High–Adult)*

CREATION ASTRONOMY DVD

DR. JASON LISLE shows from astronomy and from Genesis that God created the entire universe supernaturally, only thousands of years ago. In this illustrated lecture, Dr. Lisle reveals that when the evidence of nature is understood properly, it lines up perfectly with the clear teachings of Scripture. *36 minutes (Jr. High–Adult)*

For more information visit answersingenesis.org or visit your local bookseller.

BEGINNINGS CURRICULUM

BY STACIA MCKEEVER, ILLUSTRATED BY DAN LIETHA · Enables young students to answer foundational questions of the Christian faith, such as: • Where did God come from? • How did we get the Bible? • How old is the earth? • Did God create in six actual days? Features colorful kid-friendly handouts and a CD-ROM filled with exciting lesson illustrations. *One teacher manual, 96 pages. One complete set of six full-color student handouts. One CD-ROM with presentation illustrations. (Grades 1-5)*

THE SEVEN C'S OF HISTORY CURRICULUM

BY STACIA MCKEEVER, ILLUSTRATED BY DAN LIETHA · Updated & Expanded. Based on Ken Ham's famous teachings about creation, corruption, catastrophe, confusion, Christ, Cross and consummation. Great supplemental curriculum for homeschool, Sunday school, Christian school, family devotions and VBS. *One teacher manual, 96 pages. One complete set of seven full-color student handouts. One CD-ROM. (Grades 1-5)*

THE ORIGIN OF OLD-EARTH GEOLOGY & CHRISTIAN COMPROMISE IN THE EARLY 19TH CENTURY 2 DVDS

DR. TERRY MORTENSON · The church's compromise on biblical authority began long before Charles Darwin. This eye-opening talk by historian Terry Mortenson shows how far back biblical geologists defended biblical history (and exposed the fallacies in an old earth), but the church refused to listen. *(High School–Adult) Part 1: 53 minutes. Part 2: 70 minutes.*

THE GREAT TURNING POINT BOOK

DR. TERRY MORTENSON · Many in the church today think that "young-earth" creation is a fairly recent invention, popularized by fundamentalist Christians in the mid-20th century. AiG scholar Dr. Terry Mortenson reveals fascinating original research that documents a different story. *Softcover. 300 pages. (High School-Adult)*

For more information visit answersingenesis.org or visit your local bookseller.

FEARFULLY & WONDERFULLY MADE DVD

DR. DAVID MENTON explains from anatomical science and biology the truth of Psalm 139:13–16, which says that God weaves us together in the womb. Even more important—this acclaimed anatomist explains with grace and sensitivity the second "birth" process of salvation from John 3. *63 minutes. (Jr. High–Adult)*

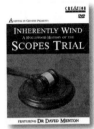

INHERENTLY WIND DVD

DR. DAVID MENTON exposes the distortions and inaccuracies in the play and movie *Inherit the Wind*, an influential propaganda piece that has deceived millions with the false belief that Christians went on a "witch hunt" to stop John Scopes from teaching evolution. In reality it was a "set up" by the American Civil Liberties Union! *74 minutes. (High School–Adult)*

THE HEARING EAR AND THE SEEING EYE DVD

DR. DAVID MENTON escorts you on a journey into the marvelous intricacies of the human ear, which has the clear stamp of the Creator and leaves skeptics speechless! *65 minutes. (High School–Adult)*

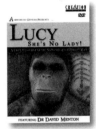

LUCY: SHE'S NO LADY DVD

DR. DAVID MENTON • Confused about the discovery of Lucy, a "missing link" between chimps and humans? Anatomist Dr. Menton leaves no doubt that the famous "Lucy" fossils belong to a knuckle-walking, apelike creature, who was not a lady! *59 minutes. (High School–Adult)*

FORMED TO FLY DVD

DR. DAVID MENTON details the amazing design features of birds. This illustrated lecture explains that the current view of bird evolution via dinosaurs is far from probable and goes against all observable evidence. *61 minutes. (High School–Adult)*

For more information visit answersingenesis.org or visit your local bookseller.

THE INTELLIGENT DESIGN MOVEMENT DVD

DR. GEORGIA PURDOM · Although many pastors and churches today are reluctant to engage the topic of creationism, some choose instead to side-step the issue by supporting Intelligent Design (ID). Dr. Purdom (Ph.D., molecular genetics) reveals the history of the ID movement and unravels the good, the bad and the ugly of this "new" idea regarding origins. Excellent for anyone entrusted with the education of children and/or families. *45 minutes. (High School–Adult)*

THE CODE OF LIFE DVD

DR. GEORGIA PURDOM explores the fascinating world of DNA and clearly shows that "junk" DNA isn't junk and that mutations and natural selection are headed in the wrong direction, corrupting and decreasing information in DNA making evolution impossible. The origin of such diversity and variability could only be the God of the Bible! *45 minutes. (High School–Adult)*

CLONING, STEM CELLS, AND THE VALUE OF LIFE DVD

MIKE RIDDLE · Human stem cells can be used to cure diseases, but are embryonic stem cells as effective as those from adults? What is the latest research on the topic? What should a Christian believe? Mike Riddle addresses the ethical issues surrounding embryonic and adult stem cell research, while deflating the myths and false reports given by the media. The value of human life is inescapable in his hard-hitting conclusion. *54 minutes. (Ages 12 and up)*

RIDDLE OF THE DINOSAURS DVD

MIKE RIDDLE · Kid-friendly animations help children learn answers to such questions as: What day did God create dinosaurs? Could you outrun a *Tyrannosaurus rex*? How many kinds of dinosaurs were there? Were dinosaurs on the Ark? And many more … . This popular AiG speaker demonstrates the use of interaction to keep students focused. *49 minutes. (Ages 5–11)*

For more information visit answersingenesis.org or visit your local bookseller.

IT'S LIKE TWO MAGAZINES IN ONE!

Use this powerful creation-based magazine to help build a Biblical Worldview in your family!

"We just received the new Answers magazine—WELL DONE!!! It is truly family-friendly and God-glorifying. Kids will love it. Adults that may be novice students will love it, and the intellectuals that like to go a lot deeper will love it. The colors, the content, and the commitment to biblical truth are all wrapped up in this magazine. I will highly recommend it."

—James Enns, Senior Pastor Rothbury Community Church, Michigan

FREE kid's magazine in every issue!

Quarterly, only $22/yr.

DEMOLISHING STRONGHOLDS DVD-BASED STUDY SERIES

Shot live before 300 teens, *Demolishing Strongholds* features cutting-edge, comic-book style animation. Use it to equip your young people to stand firm on the authority of God's Word, while challenging them to activate their faith!

Strategic topics include: • recognizing "cultural brainwashing" • developing a biblical worldview • reaching friends for Christ • engaging our evolutionized culture • learning how to be God's player in the "game" called life

This study series is excellent for youth groups, and recommended for fathers to view and discuss with their teens. Includes: twelve 30-minute DVD programs, intriguing "Man on the Street" interviews, an illustrated Leader's Guide, a Student Workbook, an integrated Bible study, and a multi-resource CD-ROM.

ANSWERS ACADEMY DVD-BASED STUDY SERIES

Are we losing an entire generation? Modern teens don't know what to believe about the Bible and Christianity. Fortunately, they earnestly want to know the truth! The purpose of the *Answers Academy* apologetics curriculum is to equip viewers of all ages to answer the questions the world is asking about the authority and accuracy of the Bible. During the thirteen illustrated lessons included in this "apologetics power pack," you will discover why it is vital to provide logical answers to skeptics, and how to give those answers with a solid understanding of what the Bible says about geology and astronomy. Viewers will learn that, contrary to popular belief, operational science runs counter to the idea of evolution and "millions of years." The facts of nature, rightly interpreted, provide an irrefutable case for the accuracy and trustworthiness of the book that claims to be the inspired word of the Creator Himself!

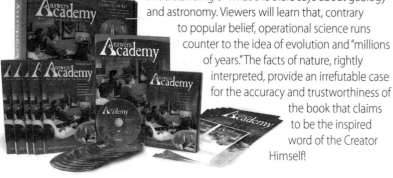

For more information visit answersingenesis.org or visit your local bookseller.